M000099750

Beautiful EMBROIDERED ACCESSORIES

EASY WAYS TO PERSONALIZE

Hats, Bandanas, Totes, Denim
and Your Favorite Clothing

LEXI MIRE BRANTMAN

founder of Mire Made Embroidery

PAGE STREET
PUBLISHING CO.

Copyright © 2020 Lexi Mire Brantman

First published in 2020 by

Page Street Publishing Co.

27 Congress Street, Suite 105

Salem, MA 01970

www.pagestreetpublishing.com

All rights reserved. No part of this book may be reproduced or used, in any form or by any means, electronic or mechanical, without prior permission in writing from the publisher.

Distributed by Macmillan, sales in Canada by The Canadian Manda Group.

24 23 22 21 20   1 2 3 4 5

ISBN-13: 978-1-64567-122-0

ISBN-10: 1-64567-122-4

Library of Congress Control Number: 2019957310

Cover and book design by Rosie Stewart for Page Street Publishing Co.

Photography by Lexi Mire Brantman

Printed and bound in China

Page Street Publishing protects our planet by donating to nonprofits like The Trustees, which focuses on local land conservation.

Dedication

This book is dedicated to anyone who has felt the tug of creative curiosity at their fingertips. The best way to get to know yourself deeply is to explore a new artistic endeavor.

Contents

INTRODUCTION   6

EMBROIDERY BASICS   8

STITCH GUIDE   11

SWEETLY STITCHED FLORAL HATS   17

Strawberry Sweethearts   21

Wildflower Magic   25

Bloomin' Cactus   29

Blossoming Alaska Wildflowers   33

California Dreamin' Poppies   37

Echinacea in Bloom   41

Mushroom Party   45

Sweet Florida Oranges   49

Happy Pink Peony   53

Unfurled Fern   57

COLORFUL AND CREATIVE BANDANAS   61

Daisy Dudes   65

Lovely Lavender   67

Mini Mushrooms   71

Red Poppy Pals   75

Lil' Lemon Slices   79

Baby Birds-of-Paradise   83

FLOWERY FANNY PACKS   87

Lush Lupine   91

Tropical Monstera   93

Radiant Sunflower   97

TOO CUTE TOTE BAGS 101

Sprouting Coffee Plant 105

Fresh Fruit 109

Colorful Succulents 113

A GARDEN OF FLORAL PATCHES 117

Snapdragon Rainbow 123

Overflowing Pothos Planter 125

Pansy Pals 129

DENIM JACKET MAGIC 133

Lush Peony 137

TEMPLATES 141

ACKNOWLEDGMENTS 172

ABOUT THE AUTHOR 173

INDEX 174

INTRODUCTION

Hi, I'm Lexi of Mire Made Embroidery, and I cannot wait to share these embroidery designs with you!

In this book you will make friends with cacti and succulents, turn plain tote bags into farmers' market necessities, make gifts for floral-obsessed loved ones and learn my signature embroidery style. You'll be able to add floral magic to any accessory, big or small. And no matter your skill level, this book is for you! Beginners will have a great time learning the ins and outs of modern embroidery, and experienced stitchers will pick up some new skills along the way.

We all have forgotten accessories that are sitting in a drawer somewhere waiting to be given new life. I will show you how to add color and interest to hats, bandanas, fanny packs, iron-on patches, totes and denim jackets. I chose accessories that are easy to find, inexpensive to purchase and are most likely already in your closet, so you can get to stitching right away! Reignite your love for your wardrobe by easily adding elegant embroidered touches and elevating your items to a new level of style.

I've always been creative in one way or another. My first creative loves were writing and photography. Hello, writing this book is my dream come true! More than three years ago, I was on Instagram on the hunt for a cute new patch for my denim jacket, when I came across a gorgeous embroidered jacket. The creative corner of my brain lit up with an excited "I can do that" attitude and I was off to the craft store for embroidery supplies. I browsed blogs, watched lots of YouTube tutorials and got lost in the sea of embroidery on Instagram. I began teaching myself traditional stitches, but I also veered off and did my own thing. I was so inspired by embroidery artists, such as Tessa Perlow and Emillie Ferris. I drew inspiration from nature, vintage botanical illustrations and the flowers that remind me of people and places I love. After adorning a few denim jackets with flowers, a friend asked me to embroider a hat for her—thank you, Katie!—and my Instagram followers absolutely loved it. My photos went viral and my follower base grew by almost 10,000 people in one month.

I began selling embroidered hats on Etsy and at art markets around my city. The response was incredible, and I sold out instantly, again and again. I realized that more people wanted embroidered hats than I was physically able to make, so I brainstormed about how to best serve my customer base. Many of my shoppers were creative souls and I realized the best product I could create for them would be an embroidery education.

I learned *so* much by creating my first embroidery pattern. It took a lot of market research and a lot of trial and error. But I had help from my amazing community of followers, and I released the pattern and learned from their feedback. My embroidery patterns got better and better. I moved on to providing embroidery kits, full of everything a crafter needed to get started. Over time, I watched the #MireMade hashtag fill up with hats made by myself and by others!

Over the last few years, I have gained over 20,000 followers, stitched over 600 hats—crazy right?!—and taught more than 350 embroidery-curious artists how to embroider. From beginners to advanced stitchers, I have received an incredible response to the way my embroidery designs are easy to follow and quick to learn. I have loved every second of this journey and can't wait to be a part of yours!

I consider myself a modern embroidery artist. Embroidery has had a serious revival in the last ten years, and it's being picked up by artists who are manipulating the medium to create meaningful pieces of modern art. Modern embroidery breaks the rules that you're used to. Traditional embroidery says to use small stitches and muted tones. Be slow, be precise and be perfect. Modern embroidery says to get messy. Make your stitches chunky and heavy, blend the colors and make them bold.

This style of embroidery embraces happy accidents and improvisations. Make mistakes and lean into them. First timers are welcomed and encouraged to dive in. Even if you've tried embroidery before, this may be a whole new experience for you! Pick up some new skills and learn how to move your embroidery from inside the hoop to out in the world on your wardrobe and accessories.

Not sure where to get started? Browse the chapters and check out the skill levels listed. Projects listed as **Beginner** are a great place to start if you're jumping into embroidery for the first time! They will familiarize you with the basic methods and stitches. Once you feel comfortable, you're ready to move on to **Intermediate**. You will add more stitches to your repertoire and work on more detailed designs. Don't be intimidated by the **Advanced** projects. The skill level is similar to Intermediate; the projects are just a bit more time consuming. Settle in with some good company or music and stitch for a while.

Don't forget to have fun with it! Enjoy creating your own works of art in my signature style—and make them your own by switching up the colors or adding new flowers in!

Lexi Mire Brantman

EMBROIDERY BASICS

You will have a great time learning how to embroider! It is going to be super easy to add a personalized touch to your items by following these instructions. These tips are general guidelines for embroidery and will be useful to refer to while working on your projects.

Each accessory you embroider on requires different materials and methods. I recommend reviewing each project before shopping. For example, I recommend a small plastic hoop for hats and fanny packs, but I like using large wooden hoops for tote bags and denim jackets.

When choosing accessories, I prefer cotton or denim materials that are soft and easy to work with. Each chapter lists my preferred item and where to find something similar. For your thread, I recommend using cotton embroidery thread. My preferred brand of thread is DMC and each project lists the colors needed.

Embroidery thread often comes out of its plastic sleeve and can quickly become unraveled and tangled. I recommend using plastic thread savers or clothespins to keep your threads organized. To use a clothespin, begin with it in the open position. Place the end of the thread into the mouth of the clothespin and allow it to close over the thread. Wrap the thread around the middle of the clothespin until you have about an inch (2.5 cm) of thread left. Tuck the end of the thread into the mouth of the clothespin, making it easy to quickly find during future use. I like to write the number of the thread on the end of the clothespin with a pen or marker.

HOW TO USE AN EMBROIDERY HOOP

Begin by separating the hoop into two pieces: the inner ring and the outer ring. The outer ring has a metal screw on top that can tighten or loosen the hoop.

Place the inner hoop on the back side of the fabric or accessory you are using. Place the outer hoop on top of the fabric and match it up with the inner hoop. Push until the two lock into place. Pull the fabric tight on the inside of the hoop and tighten the metal screw.

NEEDLE THREADING METHODS

Embroidery thread comes in skeins made up of six individual strands. In traditional embroidery, it is customary to separate the strands from one another to create thinner stitches. I prefer my stitches to look full and thick, so I recommend using all six strands of the embroidery thread for the projects in this book.

SINGLE THREAD METHOD

Using a single piece of thread is common in traditional embroidery and sewing, and you will see it occasionally in the projects in this book.

Cut about 12 to 18 inches (30 to 45 cm) of embroidery thread, keeping all six strands intact. Thread one end (a) through the needle and tie a knot onto the other end (b). Tie a second knot over the first knot to make it a little thicker and trim

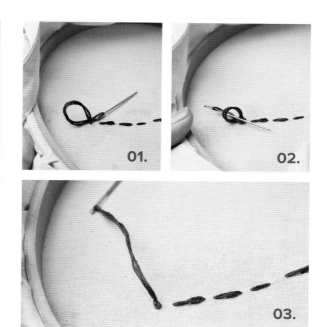

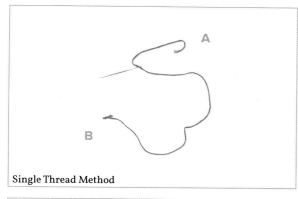

Single Thread Method

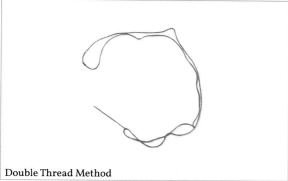

Double Thread Method

the excess thread off of the end (b). While embroidering, keep the end (a) at about a 3-inch (7.5-cm) length from the needle to prevent it from pulling out of the needle.

DOUBLE THREAD METHOD

This method is a little more challenging, as you will be doubling the number of threads in each stitch. It is my go-to and gets easier with practice. It creates stitches that are thick and have dimension. It is a common method in modern embroidery.

Cut about 18 inches (45 cm) of embroidery thread, keeping all six strands intact. Thread one end through the needle and join it with the other end. Knot the two ends together and trim the excess.

While embroidering, pull the threads taut and all the way through the fabric before creating your next stitch. The two threads may begin to spiral around each other. Twist them periodically, so they continue to be side by side.

FINISHING STITCHES

When you are near the end of your thread you will need to tie off your stitch. Do not wait until the thread is too short; do this when you have about 1½ inches (4 cm) of thread left.

01. Create a loop with your thread.

02. Feed the needle through the loop to create a knot.

03. Pull tight and cut the excess thread.

STITCH GUIDE

Time to learn some stitches! These are my favorite because they are super easy to learn and will pop on any fabric or color.

There are many embroidery stitches out there! If you know any that aren't in this book and you want to incorporate them into your design, have at it. If something isn't working out, don't be afraid to cut out a stitch and start over. These designs are so special because they're made to be played with and personalized.

BACKSTITCH

The backstitch is used to create lines in your embroidery design. This stitch will be the primary way you create stems in these embroidery projects. My backstitch method is a little different than the traditional technique.

01. Begin by coming up from the back of the hoop with the needle and create a single stitch that is about the length of your pinky nail.

02. Then, once again come up from the back of the hoop and insert the needle about ½ inch (1.3 cm) down the stem line.

03. Bring the needle and thread all the way through, pull it taut and insert it into the center of your first stitch.

04. Repeat this until the length of your line is complete, always inserting the needle into the center of the previous stitch.

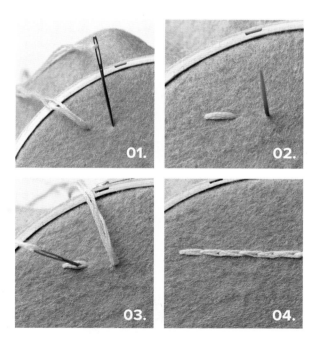

DAISY SHAPE METHOD (SIDE VIEW)

I use daisies in most of my designs because they are cute, colorful and easily recognizable. Daisies in varying sizes add depth and dimension to any embroidery composition.

01. Create the daisy flower by stitching 4 to 6 lines in a radiating shape. I try to keep this shape at about a 90-degree angle to create an arrow shape.

02. Use a single stitch to create the pollen, which overlaps the intersection of the petal threads. This is usually done with yellow, orange or brown thread.

03. When adding a stem to the daisy, use the backstitch to create a simple line and a single stitch to create a small leaf.

DAISY SHAPE METHOD (FRONT VIEW)

In some of the designs, it is more visually dynamic to stitch the daises from the front view. Feel free to incorporate these any time the tutorial encourages you to improvise.

01. Use 7 to 9 stitches to create the daisy petals. The stitches should meet at one center point and be about the same length.

02. Create the pollen by overlapping the center point a few times until you create a circular shape.

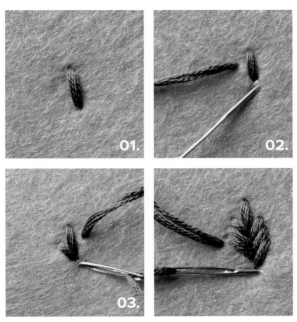

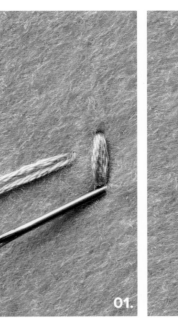

FISHBONE STITCH

The fishbone stitch is used to create leaves and flower petals.

01. Begin with a single line at the tip of the petal or leaf. This is your base stitch.

02. Create an arrow shape by making alternating single stitches on each side of the base stitch, left, right, left, right, each meeting slightly below the bottom of the base stitch.

03. Always start each new stitch from the top of the leaf and bring it down diagonally, right below your previous stitch.

FLORAL BUD STITCH

This tiny flower is created using a simplified version of the fishbone stitch. Use the floral bud stitch to add color and complexity to any design!

01. Begin with a single line at the tip of the petal or leaf. This is your base stitch.

02. Create an arrow shape by stitching 1 line on each side of the base stitch.

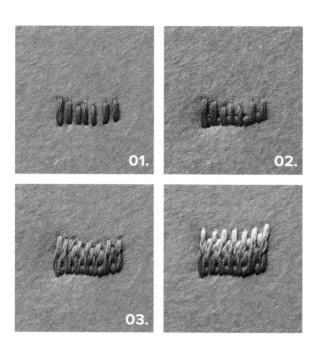

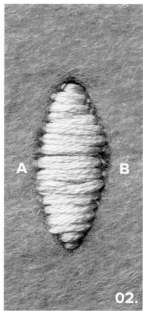

LONG AND SHORT STITCH

The long and short stitch is an embroidery technique used to create value in an embroidery design. My use of it is a bit of a variation on the traditional method.

01. Create a series of stitches that are around the same length about a thread's width apart from one another.

02. Fill between these stitches with slightly shorter stitches to create a staggered effect.

03. Continue adding to the design in the same method, overlapping the previous stitch row to blend the threads and the colors.

SATIN STITCH

The satin stitch is used to fill in shapes. It is a very uniform stitch that appears clean because it is created using parallel lines.

01. Fill in your shape using parallel stitches side by side.

02. Always start your stitches on the same side of the shape (side A) and end on the other side (side B). Twisting tends to happen when you use the Double Thread Method; periodically rotate the needle to keep the thread flat.

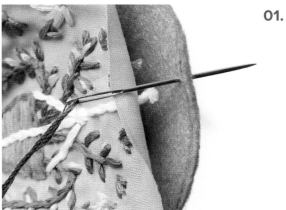

01.

03.

02.

WHIPSTITCH

The whipstitch is used to attach patches. It is typically used with two pieces of fabric. This stitch can be done close together or with space between the stitches, whatever you prefer stylistically.

01. Begin with your two fabrics held together. Separate the top edges and insert the needle between the fabric. Push the needle through the back fabric only, close to the top edge. This will hide the knot as you embroider.

02. Insert the needle into the front fabric as close to the knot as you can get. This time bring the needle through both fabric swatches. You have your first stitch!

03. Continue stitching small stitches in this way, always bringing the thread over the top edge of the fabrics and going through both layers of fabric in uniform lines.

Sweetly Stitched FLORAL HATS

Embroidered hats are my bread and butter as an embroidery artist. They are what I am best known for and are always a treat for me to create. I have a passion for taking objects typically worn out of utility and turning them into works of art. I love that anything can be infused with creativity and meaning, hats included!

In this chapter, I'll show you how to transform your favorite baseball cap into a personalized, stylish accessory that shows off your embroidery skills. You will create pieces of wearable art that are bright and unique. You are learning a new skill and you're also creating your new favorite adventure gear! From hiking to beach days, an embroidered hat will look amazing and keep you cool.

This chapter includes some of my absolute favorite designs, featuring sweet Florida oranges (page 49), happy pink peonies (page 53) and silly little mushrooms (page 45). Have a blast and feel free to add a personal touch to everything you do!

TIPS FOR CHOOSING A HAT

I recommend using a 6-panel cotton baseball cap without an inside liner. Hats with any netting or lining inside will not work with the pattern transfer method in this book. I prefer pigment-dyed hats because they have a faded, washed-looking color. Cotton hats are especially perfect for embroidery. You can wear them day in and day out unlike a top or dress, and they're super durable, so the embroidery stays pristine for longer.

I also recommend choosing hats in lighter colors when using my patterns. It is more difficult for light to pass through dark hats, such as black or navy blue, and light is necessary for the pattern transfer method.

Hat brands I use often are Authentic Pigment, Anvil and Comfort Colors.

ATTACHING AN EMBROIDERY HOOP TO A HAT

You will use an embroidery hoop for every project in this chapter. In some images, the hats are displayed without a hoop, in order to fully present the embroidery technique for each project step. The steps should still be executed with a hoop attached unless otherwise instructed.

Begin by separating the hoop into two pieces, the inner ring and the outer ring. The outer ring has a metal screw on top that can tighten or loosen the hoop.

Place the inner hoop on the inside of the hat. Place the outer hoop on the outside of the hat and match it up with the inner hoop. Push until the two lock into place. Pull the fabric tight on the inside of the hoop and tighten the metal screw. You may need to pull hard to get a flat stitching surface; the hats are durable and will be fine.

HAT PATTERN TRANSFER TUTORIAL

Cut out the designated pattern templates from the back of the book. Each project will have two to three cutouts. Cut close to the design; there is no need to leave a lot of space on the edges.

01. Apply the hoop to the hat according to my instructions.

02. Place shape I face down on the inside of the hat. Make sure your design is where you want it and tape it to the inside of the hat. Be sure to pull back the sweatband of the hat during the transfer process because it will block out any light.

03. Use a flashlight or cell phone light to illuminate the inside of the hat.

04. Transfer your pattern using a water-soluble marker. It's okay if you make mistakes; you will remove leftover marks at the end. It is easiest to see the lines if the paper is pressed firmly against the hat and you are in a dark room. The part of your pattern that overlaps on the seam will be hard to see and may need to be added after you finish transferring the rest of the design. Keep the book open to the project page; if you are having trouble seeing certain elements, freehand them instead.

05. Once you are done with shape 1, move on to shape 2. Look at the main image of the project to determine where the pieces fit together. Repeat steps 2 through 4 with all the remaining shapes. Once you have transferred all of the shapes to the hat, you are ready to embroider.

06. To remove the lines after embroidering, use a cotton swab dipped in water and blot the visible blue lines. If the ink does not immediately disappear, submerge the spot in water and let the hat air-dry.

HAT TIPS

Keep the fabric tight. As you stitch, check the tightness of the fabric. Pull on the fabric on the outside edge of the hoop every so often to create a flat surface inside the hoop.

Keep the thread tight. After every stitch, pull the thread taut so that the stitches aren't loose. The thread may twist; just keep an eye on it. Rotate the needle to untwist it if it is affecting your stitches.

Make it your own! Every design can be added to in your own special way.

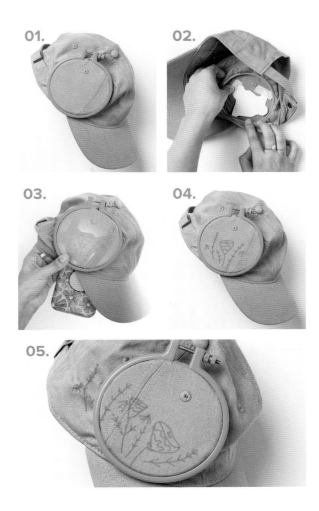

strawberry
SWEETHEARTS

There is nothing like picking a fresh strawberry off of the plant and eating it while it's still warm from the summer sunshine. This hat is dedicated to fruit lovers who want some protection from the UV rays while working in the garden or visiting their favorite you-pick farm. In this project, you will jump right into learning how to stitch stems, leaves and small flowers—all skills you will use throughout the whole book! You'll also learn how to embroider strawberries, which you can add to any article of clothing to make it more playful. I love embroidering strawberries on khaki or agave green hats so that the red really pops! This design also includes white strawberry flowers.

LEVEL: BEGINNER

MATERIALS

Khaki or green pigment-dyed hat (Pictured is Authentic Pigment brand in Khaki.)

Template (page 141)

Water-soluble marker

Tape

4-inch (10-cm) plastic embroidery hoop

Size 18 chenille needle

Embroidery scissors

EMBROIDERY THREAD COLORS

Light green (DMC 906)

Dark red (DMC 815)

Light red (DMC 666)

White (DMC 3865)

Light yellow (DMC 743)

Light purple (DMC 211) (optional)

01.

02.

03.

04.

EMBROIDER!

01. Transfer the pattern onto the hat using the method from the beginning of the chapter (page 18). This entire project will be created using the Double Thread Method (page 9).

02. Stitch the stems with your light green embroidery thread. Start at the base of the stems and use the backstitch (page 11). At the top of each strawberry stem, stitch 2 single stitches in a V shape. Use the fishbone stitch (page 13) to create the leaves.

03. Fill in each strawberry using the long and short stitch (page 14). Begin with the dark red thread and fill in the bottom right side of each strawberry.

04. Switch to the light red thread to complete the shape. Use the white thread in single stitches to create the seeds.

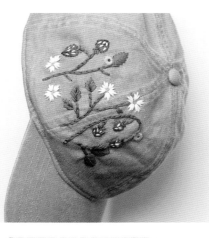

05.

07.

06.

05. Continue using the white thread to create the front-facing strawberry flowers. Use a floral bud stitch (page 13) to create each flower petal. Be sure to leave a circle in the center for the pollen to be added.

06. To create the white flowers that are at a side angle, use the daisy shape method (page 12) with 4 to 6 stitches. Switch to the light yellow thread to add the pollen. For the sideways flowers, use a single stitch for the pollen. For the front-facing flowers, stitch the pollen using 1 to 2 stitches side by side.

07. You are done stitching the pattern, but you can keep going! Add small floral buds in light yellow and light purple in the empty spaces of the design. Add as many or as few as you'd like in varying sizes. I love using these filler flowers to make the design feel full and colorful. Remove the hoop to add flowers below the design.

08. Remove the water-soluble marker lines, as described on page 19. Your hat is ready to be worn!

Wildflower
MAGIC

Bluebonnets, snapdragons and lavender, OH MY! Don't these little blooms just make you want to unfurl a picnic blanket and have a snack in the sunshine? I live in Florida and these magic wild varieties don't pop up in my daily life often. So rather than enjoying them fresh, I get so much joy out of stitching them and trying to do justice to their beauty. In this project, you will be playing with color! I love adding a rainbow of color to a vibrant hat, such as this pink one. I try to choose colors with varying values, so there is contrast in the design. This design also includes white and light purple daisies, a small Queen Anne's lace flower and some imaginary blooms.

LEVEL: BEGINNER

MATERIALS

Pink or yellow pigment-dyed hat (Pictured is Authentic Pigment brand in Flamingo.)

Template (page 141)

Water-soluble marker

Tape

4-inch (10-cm) plastic embroidery hoop

Size 18 chenille needle

Embroidery scissors

EMBROIDERY THREAD COLORS

Medium green (DMC 3818)

Medium purple (DMC 552)

Light yellow (DMC 743)

White (DMC 3865)

Dark dusty pink (DMC 3350)

Medium magenta (DMC 3326)

Light pink (DMC 818)

Dark blue (DMC 820)

Medium blue (DMC 3843)

Light blue (DMC 747)

Light purple (DMC 554)

Dark orange (DMC 900)

Light orange (DMC 741)

01.

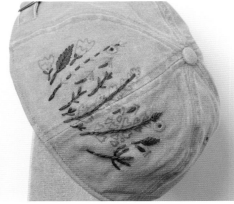

02.

03.

04.

EMBROIDER!

01. Transfer the pattern onto the hat using the method from the beginning of the chapter (page 18). This entire project will be created using the Double Thread Method (page 9).

02. Stitch the stems with your medium green embroidery thread, using the backstitch (page 11) and starting at the base of the stem. Some of the stems end in a V shape at the top. The lavender stem is created using single stitches in the spaces between the floral elements in a dashed line. Use the fishbone stitch (page 13) to create the leaves and the top of the bluebonnet.

03. Each lavender flower is created by using the floral bud stitch (page 13) with the medium purple thread. Create the yellow sprigs and the white Queen Anne's lace flowers with 2 stitches in a V shape on the tip of each stem, using the light yellow and white threads, respectively.

04. The snapdragon is made up of the dark dusty pink, medium magenta and light pink threads. Using 3 to 4 stitches, fill in each flower shape with stitches angled down and in toward the stem. Add a light yellow stitch to the center of each flower.

05.

06.

07.

05. Use the floral bud stitch to create the bluebonnet flowers. Begin at the bottom of the stem with the dark blue thread and transition to medium blue, followed by light blue. Switch to the white and then light purple threads to create the daisies using the daisy shape method (page 12). Switch to the light yellow thread and stitch the flower pollen.

06. The two-toned orange flowers are created by using the dark and light orange threads and the long and short stitch (page 14). Begin with dark orange thread and stitch a fan shape, leaving gaps between the threads. Use the light orange to fill in the gaps and overlap the ends of the darker thread. Add pollen using the light yellow thread to make 2 single stitches in a V shape.

07. You are done stitching the pattern, but you can keep going! Add small floral buds in light yellow, light orange and light blue in the empty spaces of the design. Add as many or as few as you'd like in varying sizes. I love using these filler flowers to make the design feel full and colorful. Remove the hoop to add flowers below the design.

08. Remove the water-soluble marker lines, as described on page 19. Your hat is ready to be worn!

CACTUS

Cacti are having a moment. These prickly friends have long been ignored and now they are finally having their much-deserved time in the sun! I love these pokey guys because they are incredibly easy to keep alive—and when you catch one in bloom, it's pure magic! This project is so exciting because it's your first foray into a large embroidered shape rather than small flowers and leaves. In big designs like this, I always place the flower or plant in the center of one of the hat panels, rather than on the seam, so it is easier to stitch. Be sure to keep your fabric tight within the hoop, tugging the edges periodically to maintain the tension. This design also includes pink daisies and desert larkspur.

LEVEL: BEGINNER

MATERIALS

Moss green or orange pigment-dyed hat (Pictured is Comfort Colors brand in Moss.)

Template (page 143)

Water-soluble marker

Tape

4-inch (10-cm) plastic embroidery hoop

Size 18 chenille needle

Embroidery scissors

EMBROIDERY THREAD COLORS

Light green (DMC 3851)

Dark emerald green (DMC 909)

White (DMC 3865)

Dark blue (DMC 820)

Medium blue (DMC 3760)

Light blue (DMC 157)

Dark orange (DMC 900)

Medium orange (DMC 946)

Light orange (DMC 741)

Light yellow (DMC 743)

Medium pink (DMC 3354)

Light purple (DMC 211) (optional)

Dark dusty pink (DMC 3350) (optional)

01.

02.

03.

04.

EMBROIDER!

01. Transfer the pattern onto the hat using the method from the beginning of the chapter (page 18). This entire project will be created using the Double Thread Method (page 9). I placed the pattern closer to the front of the hat so the cactus can take up a whole panel, rather than stitching it on a seam.

02. Stitch the larkspur stems, starting at the base, using your light green embroidery thread and the backstitch (page 11). Switch to the dark emerald green thread and continue with the backstitch to outline the cactus. Use multiple single stitches to create the base of the cactus bud and flower bloom.

03. Begin at the base of the cactus and with the light green thread, use the backstitch to create vertical lines filling in the cactus shape. Switch to the white thread to create V shapes along the lines of the cactus. Now your cactus is prickly!

04. The larkspur is made up of the dark blue, medium blue and light blue threads. Using 4 to 6 stitches, fill in each flower shape with dark blue stitches angled down and in toward the stem. As you move up the stem, switch to the medium blue and then the light blue. Create the top flower using a fishbone stitch (page 13).

05.

06.

07.

08.

05. To create the cactus flower, begin with the dark orange thread. Using the long and short stitch (page 14), fill in the bottom of the flower with varying long and short lines. Stitch a line of short stitches side by side along the top edge of the flower.

06. Switch to the medium orange and continue the long and short stitch method, overlapping the dark orange thread to blend the colors. Complete the petal, in light orange, filling between the medium orange lines but keeping the top of the petal clean and uniform. Use a few light yellow stitches to create the pollen and to add a highlight effect to the top of the petal over the light orange.

07. To create the cactus bud, use the dark orange thread and create a fan shape. Switch to the light orange thread to fill in the bud using the long and short stitch. Add a few stitches of light yellow to create a highlight. Complete the daisies with the medium pink thread using the daisy shape method (page 12). Use a single light yellow stitch for the pollen.

08. You are done stitching the pattern, but you can keep going! Add as many or as few small floral buds (page 13) as desired in light purple and dark dusty pink in the empty spaces of the design. Remove the hoop to add flowers below the design.

09. Remove the water-soluble marker lines, as described on page 19. Your hat is ready to be worn!

Blossoming
ALASKA WILDFLOWERS

This design is extra close to my heart! Alaska is a very special place to me, full of incredible memories of time spent in lush nature with my husband and our family. These beautiful blooms remind me of my trips to this wild place. I love this project because it looks complex, but it is actually super simple to stitch. You will look like an embroidery expert when you wear this hat out in the world. This design will give you more experience with tiny, detailed flowers, which will be super useful when embroidering bandanas. This design includes fireweed, lupine, forget-me-nots, yarrow and bluebells.

LEVEL: BEGINNER

MATERIALS

Yellow or blue pigment-dyed hat (Pictured is Authentic Pigment brand in Mustard.)

Template (page 143)

Water-soluble marker

Tape

4-inch (10-cm) plastic embroidery hoop

Size 18 chenille needle

Embroidery scissors

EMBROIDERY THREAD COLORS

Dark green (DMC 895)

Dark indigo (DMC 550)

Indigo (DMC 333)

White (DMC 3865)

Light blue (DMC 828)

Medium yellow (DMC 725)

Dark magenta (DMC 917)

Medium magenta (DMC 961)

Light orange (DMC 3853) (optional)

Light pink (DMC 894) (optional)

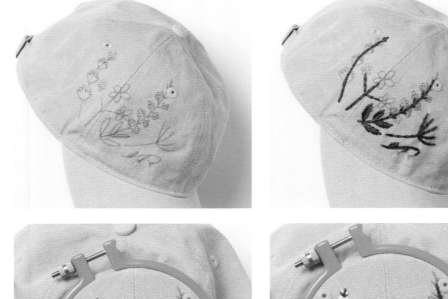

01.

02.

03.

04.

EMBROIDER!

01. Transfer the pattern onto the hat using the method from the beginning of the chapter (page 18). This entire project will be created using the Double Thread Method (page 9).

02. Stitch the stems with your dark green embroidery thread. Start at the base of the stems and use the backstitch (page 11). Use single stitches in a V shape to create the small stems on the stalk of the fireweed (the tall stalk with pink flowers). Create the leaves and the tip of the lupine using the fishbone stitch (page 13).

03. The lupine is made up of the dark indigo, indigo and white threads, using the satin stitch (page 14). Begin with dark indigo thread, filling in the two shapes at the bottom of the lupine, and then switch to indigo thread for the remaining two shapes. Add a white stitch to the center of each flower. Add 4 to 6 single stitches of white thread to the tip of the stem, overlapping the green thread.

04. Create the forget-me-not petals using the light blue thread and the satin stitch. Add a short white stitch between each petal. Use the medium yellow thread to create a few single stitches for the pollen.

05.

06.

07.

08.

05. Begin the fireweed with the dark magenta thread. Work up the stem, stitching the flowers in a daisy shape (page 12). Halfway up the stem, switch to the medium magenta thread and complete the smaller flowers and buds. Use the floral bud stitch (page 13) to complete the tip of the fireweed stem.

06. The yarrow flowers are made with the floral bud stitch using the white thread.

07. Switch to the dark indigo thread to create the bluebells. Fill in the bell shapes using the long and short stitch (page 14). At the bottom of each flower, add a few stitches of indigo angled upward.

08. You are done stitching the pattern, but you can keep going! Add small floral buds in light orange, white and light pink in the empty spaces of the design. Add as many or as few as you'd like in varying sizes. I love using these filler flowers to make the design feel full and colorful. Remove the hoop to add flowers below the design.

09. Remove the water-soluble marker lines, as described on page 19. Your hat is ready to be worn!

California Dreamin' POPPIES

California poppies are a crowd favorite, and I have fallen in love with them as I have been asked to stitch them again and again. These blooms are the California state flower and are often called California sunlight or a "cup of gold" flowers. They light up fields when they bloom in the summer with their radiant yellow petals. I love that this design is so colorful and playful, and it's the perfect summer birthday gift for a California lover. This project will give you more experience blending colors with the long and short stitch. Remember to make it your own; it doesn't have to be as structured as it may seem. Overlap, run colors together, and paint with your thread! This design also includes lavender and a simple blue lupine.

LEVEL: INTERMEDIATE

MATERIALS

Blue or khaki pigment-dyed hat (Pictured is Authentic Pigment brand in Bay.)

Template (page 145)

Water-soluble marker

Tape

4-inch (10-cm) plastic embroidery hoop

Size 18 chenille needle

Embroidery scissors

EMBROIDERY THREAD COLORS

Dark hunter green (DMC 3345)

Medium purple (DMC 552)

Dark blue (DMC 820)

Medium blue (DMC 3843)

Light blue (DMC 747)

Dark orange (DMC 900)

Light orange (DMC 3853)

Medium yellow (DMC 725)

Light yellow (DMC 726)

Light pink (DMC 352) (optional)

Magenta (DMC 3731) (optional)

01.

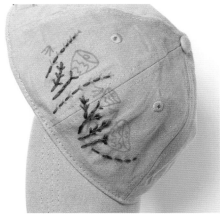

02.

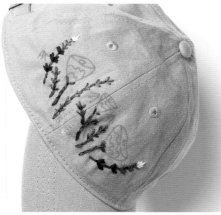

03.

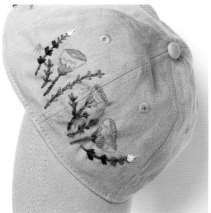

04.

EMBROIDER!

01. Transfer the pattern onto the hat using the method from the beginning of the chapter (page 18). This entire project will be created using the Double Thread Method (page 9).

02. Stitch at the base of the stems with your dark hunter green embroidery thread using the backstitch (page 11). Create the lavender and lupine stems by adding single stitches in the spaces between the flower petals. Add the leaves using 2 stitches in a V shape.

03. Each lavender flower is created with the medium purple thread using the floral bud stitch (page 13). Overlap the green thread as needed. The lupine flowers are created by using 2 to 4 stitches in a V shape beginning with dark blue, then transitioning to medium blue and then light blue. Complete the top of the stem with a light blue fishbone stitch (page 13).

04. Use the dark orange thread and the long and short stitch (page 14) to begin the poppy flowers. After completing the bottom of each poppy flower, use the same thread to create short stitches side by side to represent the inside of the flower.

05.

06.

07.

05. Continue the poppy flower with light orange thread and using the same method. Overlap the bottom dark orange thread to blend the colors. Switch to the medium yellow thread and create the top edge of the flower petals, overlapping the light orange thread.

06. Go back in with the dark orange thread and create a line or two on each flower with the backstitch to create the suggestion of multiple petals. Create the pollen using the light yellow in a W shape. Continue with the light yellow thread to create the daisy flowers (page 12). Use the dark orange thread to create the daisy pollen.

07. You are done stitching the pattern, but you can keep going! Add small floral buds in light pink and magenta in the empty spaces of the design. Add as many or as few as you'd like in varying sizes. I love using these filler flowers to make the design feel full and colorful. Remove the hoop to add flowers below the design.

08. Remove the water-soluble marker lines, as described on page 19. Your hat is ready to be worn!

Echinacea
IN BLOOM

Echinacea, also known as coneflower, is an incredible plant! It is believed to have many health benefits and is also a delicious addition to your tea collection. They like to pop up in meadows and are often visited by curious bees and butterflies. I like them because their vivid pink color is one I rarely see—it feels extra special to get to use them in a design! They're almost too bright to capture with a camera, but they're perfect for painting with thread! I suggest playing around with the placement of the designs on the hats. This one, for example, would look lovely across the front of the hat as well! This design also includes small purple buds and yellow floral sprigs.

LEVEL: INTERMEDIATE

MATERIALS

Orange or green pigment-dyed hat (Pictured is Authentic Pigment brand in Yam.)

Template (page 145)

Water-soluble marker

Tape

4-inch (10-cm) plastic embroidery hoop

Size 18 chenille needle

Embroidery scissors

EMBROIDERY THREAD COLORS

Dark green (DMC 986)

Medium yellow (DMC 725)

Dark brown (DMC 898)

Medium orange (DMC 946)

Dark magenta (DMC 600)

Light magenta (DMC 603)

Medium purple (DMC 552)

White (DMC 3865) (optional)

Medium blue (DMC 798) (optional)

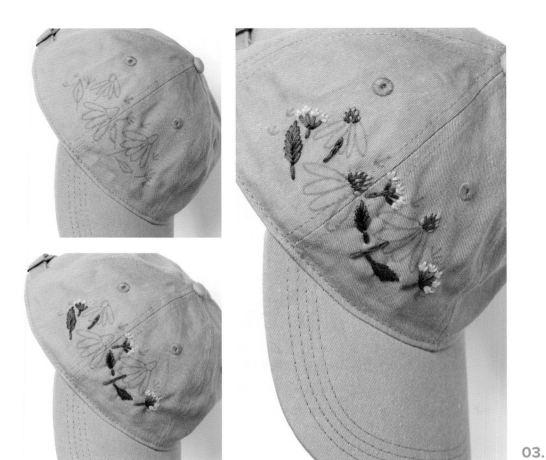

01.

02.

03.

EMBROIDER!

01. Transfer the pattern onto the hat using the method from the beginning of the chapter (page 18). This entire project will be created using the Double Thread Method (page 9).

02. Stitch the stems, starting at the base, using your dark green embroidery thread and the backstitch (page 11). For the leaves, use the fishbone stitch (page 13). Use the medium yellow thread and the floral bud stitch (page 13) to complete the yellow floral sprigs.

03. Begin the echinacea flowers with the dark brown thread. Create the cone shape using the satin stitch (page 14). Switch to the medium orange thread and add small, single stitches all over the cone to create the pollen texture.

04.

05.

06.

04. The echinacea flower petals are created using the dark and light magenta threads with the long and short stitch (page 14). Begin by creating the base of each petal with the dark magenta thread, overlapping the threads and staying uniform.

05. Continue the echinacea petals by switching to the light magenta thread. Overlap the dark magenta threads to blend the colors and round off the tip of each petal. Switch to the medium purple thread and create buds using the floral bud stitch.

06. You are done stitching the pattern, but you can keep going! Add small floral buds in white and medium blue in the empty spaces of the design. Add as many or as few as you'd like in varying sizes. I love using these filler flowers to make the design feel full and colorful. Remove the hoop to add flowers below the design.

07. Remove the water-soluble marker lines, as described on page 19. Your hat is ready to be worn!

PARTY

I love stitching mushrooms. They are so diverse and come in so many fun shapes and colors. My favorite is the classic fly agaric mushroom, also known as a toadstool, with the red cap covered in white spots. I just can't help but imagine little critters and fairies hanging out under there in a rainstorm like it's nature's cutest umbrella. Make this design for your shroom-loving friend, for yourself or make one for each of you! I like this project because it is more neutral in color and subject matter than some of the others. It's perfect for someone who doesn't wear a ton of bright colors or who prefers plants over flowers. I stitched this design on the side of my hat, but I think it would also look beautiful across the front of a hat.

LEVEL: INTERMEDIATE

MATERIALS

Khaki or green pigment-dyed hat (Pictured is Authentic Pigment brand in Khaki with Willow brim.)

Template (page 145)

Water-soluble marker

Tape

4-inch (10-cm) plastic embroidery hoop

Size 18 chenille needle

Embroidery scissors

EMBROIDERY THREAD COLORS

Light green (DMC 470)

Medium brown (DMC 301)

Light brown (DMC 729)

Dark red (DMC 815)

Medium red (DMC 349)

White (DMC 3865)

Medium yellow (DMC 725) (optional)

Indigo (DMC 333) (optional)

01.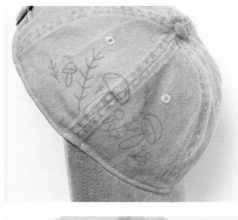

02.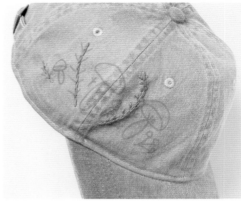

03.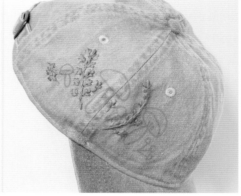

04.

EMBROIDER!

01. Transfer the pattern onto the hat using the method from the beginning of the chapter (page 18). This entire project will be created using the Double Thread Method (page 9).

02. Stitch the stems with your light green embroidery thread. Start at the base of the stems and use the backstitch (page 11). The small green leaves on the sprig on the right are created with stitches in a V shape down the length of the stem and 3 stitches for the tip.

03. Use the floral bud stitch (page 13) to create leaves on the stems on the left side of the design and for the small leaves throughout the design.

04. Begin the mushroom on the left and use the medium brown thread. Fill in the underside of the cap, radiating the stitches in a fan shape from the tip of the stem. Switch to the light brown thread and use the long and short stitch (page 14) to fill in the stem and cap. Continue with the light brown to fill in the next small mushroom with the long and short stitch.

05.

06.

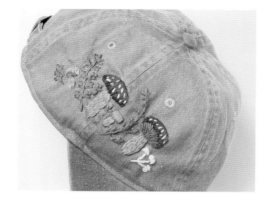

07.

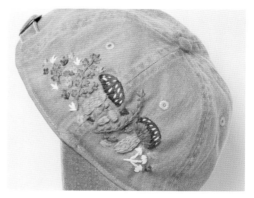

08.

05. To create the red mushroom on the right, begin with the medium brown thread and stitch under the cap in a radiating shape. Use the long and short stitch to create the stems of both red mushrooms with the light brown thread. Switch to the dark red and fill in the bottom half of each mushroom cap with the long and short stitch.

06. Finish the red mushroom caps with the medium red color using the long and short stitch. Make sure the stitches go along the edge of the shape so it is clean and uniform. Switch to the white thread and create small random dots using single stitches to make the mushrooms appear spotted.

07. The small white mushrooms are created using the white thread and the backstitch. Stitch the caps using the satin stitch (page 14).

08. You are done stitching the pattern, but you can keep going! Add small floral buds in white, medium yellow and indigo in the empty spaces of the design. Add as many or as few as you'd like in varying sizes to make the design feel full and colorful. Remove the hoop to add flowers below the design.

09. Remove the water-soluble marker lines, as described on page 19. Your hat is ready to be worn!

Sweet Florida
ORANGES

I'm a Florida girl and nothing, I mean NOTHING, says Florida like eating
a fresh orange. We had multiple citrus trees in our backyard growing up,
including oranges and grapefruits. I have such vivid memories of plucking
an orange from the tree and peeling it while sprawled out in the grass under
the warm Florida sun. In this project, you will have the chance to use the long
and short stitch in a new way. Rather than creating straight lines, you will be
stitching in a spiral shape. You will see how blending the threads together can
create dimension and volume. This strategy applies to creating other citrus
as well. After this, try your hand at a lemon or a grapefruit! This design also
includes an orange slice and orange blossoms.

LEVEL: ADVANCED

MATERIALS

Green or khaki pigment-dyed hat (Pictured is
Authentic Pigment brand in Willow.)

Template (page 147)

Water-soluble marker

Tape

4-inch (10-cm) plastic embroidery hoop

Size 18 chenille needle

Embroidery scissors

EMBROIDERY THREAD COLORS

Lime green (DMC 907)

White (DMC 3865)

Medium yellow (DMC 725)

Dark orange (DMC 900)

Medium orange (DMC 946)

Light orange (DMC 741)

Medium purple (DMC 552) (optional)

Medium pink (DMC 602) (optional)

01.

02.

03.

04.

EMBROIDER!

01. Transfer the pattern onto the hat using the method from the beginning of the chapter (page 18). This entire project will use the Double Thread Method (page 9). Place the pattern closer to the front of the hat so that the orange can take up a whole panel, rather than stitching it on a seam.

02. Stitch the base of the stems with your lime green embroidery thread and using the backstitch (page 11). The stem of the main orange is made up of 2 lines side by side. Use the fishbone stitch (page 13) to create the leaves.

03. Each orange blossom is created with white thread using 6 stitches: 4 for the petals and 2 in a V shape on top. Create the yellow pollen with 2 stitches between the white V shape.

04. The orange is created using dark orange, medium orange and light orange thread. Outline the bottom left edge of the circle in the dark orange thread with 2 lines using the backstitch. The stitches should create a curved line. Gradually fill in the bottom of the orange using the long and short stitch (page 14), continuing along the curve of the orange. Let the stitches overlap one another and leave some single stitches to overlap with the next color.

05.

06.

07.

08.

05. Begin with the medium orange thread, outlining the rest of the orange shape with the backstitch. With the long and short stitch, work toward the center of the orange gradually in a spiral pattern. The stitches should be curving inward, to create dimension in the orange. When there is approximately 2 x 2 inches (5 x 5 cm) of blank space left in the center of the shape, switch to the light orange thread to finish the orange.

06. Continue spiraling inward with the long and short stitch until you reach the final gap of space. Fill that in with a few stitches side by side. Go back in with the various orange threads to blend the colors a little more. Add medium orange into the dark orange area and light orange into the medium orange area, overlapping stitches like paint strokes to create a blended quality.

07. To create the orange slice, stitch the orange peel with the medium orange thread, using a backstitch. Create 3 lines side by side. Switch to the white thread and continue with the backstitch to outline the inside of the orange peel, the 3 white lines and the outside edge of the fruit. Complete the slice by using the medium orange thread and the long and short stitch to fill in the triangular shapes.

08. You are done stitching the pattern, but you can keep going! Add as many small floral buds in medium yellow, medium purple and medium pink in the empty spaces of the design as desired. Remove the hoop to add flowers below the design.

09. Remove the water-soluble marker lines, as described on page 19. Your hat is ready to be worn!

Happy
PINK PEONY

One of my absolute favorite flowers to spot in a wedding bouquet is a bright pink peony. They are stunning and fragrant as heck! I have always loved seeing them portrayed in watercolor paintings or immortalized in ink in a tattoo. I wanted to try them when I started my embroidery journey, but I was always so intimidated by their layers of petals. After stitching them a few different ways, I found a method that is super easy to learn and execute! You'll be making a gorgeous peony in no time. Soon enough, you'll be adding peonies to everything! This design also includes purple daisies and small pink buds.

LEVEL: ADVANCED

MATERIALS

Green or blue pigment-dyed hat (Pictured is Authentic Pigment brand in Willow.)

Template (page 147)

Water-soluble marker

Tape

4-inch (10-cm) plastic embroidery hoop

Size 18 chenille needle

Embroidery scissors

EMBROIDERY THREAD COLORS

Light green (DMC 471)

Light purple (DMC 554)

Medium yellow (DMC 725)

Dark dusty pink (DMC 3350)

Red (DMC 816)

Medium magenta (DMC 3326)

Light pink (DMC 818)

Dark orange (DMC 900) (optional)

01.

02.

03.

04.

EMBROIDER!

01. Transfer the pattern onto the hat using the method from the beginning of the chapter (page 18). This entire project will be created using the Double Thread Method (page 9). Place the pattern closer to the front of the hat so the peony can take up a whole panel, rather than stitching it on a seam.

02. Using the backstitch (page 11), stitch the stems in the light green thread, beginning at the base. The small green leaves are created by adding 2 stitches in a V shape down the length of each stem. Complete the top of the stems with the floral bud stitch (page 13). Create the daisy leaves with 1 to 2 single stitches as needed.

03. The light purple daises are made using the daisy shape method (page 12) with the medium yellow thread for the pollen. The small pink buds are made using the floral bud stitch with the dark dusty pink thread and a single medium yellow stitch in the center for the pollen.

04. The peony is made up of 3 petals using the red, dark dusty pink, medium magenta and light pink. Using the long and short stitch (page 14) and the red thread, fill in the shape at the base of the flower and curve around the outside edges of the flower to create a rounded edge. Create the inside of the flower, at the top of the design, using the satin stitch (page 14). Use short stitches side by side, fully filling in the area.

05.

06.

07.

08.

05. Continue the peony with the dark dusty pink thread, overlapping the dark pink thread to blend the colors. Use a few stitches in a backstitch to outline the inside edges of the petals to distinguish them from one another.

06. Switch to the medium magenta thread and continue with the same method, moving further up the petals. Overlap the thread colors to create a blended, painterly look.

07. Continuing with the long and short stitch, use the light pink thread to finish each petal, keeping the top of the petals clean and uniform. Overlap the medium magenta thread to create a highlight effect. Use the backstitch to create a line between the petals to distinguish them from one another. Use 5 medium yellow stitches in a radiating shape to create the pollen.

08. You are done stitching the pattern, but you can keep going! Add as many small floral buds in medium yellow and dark orange in the empty spaces of the design as desired. Remove the hoop to add flowers below the design.

09. Remove the water-soluble marker lines, as described on page 19. Your hat is ready to be worn!

Unfurled
FERN

Big, lush ferns brushing against your boots on a long hike are such a welcome greeting from nature. Ferns remind me of forest floors in Florida and Alaska—two very different places that are home to the same lovely green buddy. This design is inspired by the Pacific Northwest, home to ferns, Indian paintbrush and lily of the valley. This project has a soft, jewel-toned color scheme, which means it is perfect for anyone's wardrobe. It matches everything! It is the perfect gift for someone who loves hiking and being outside.

LEVEL: ADVANCED

MATERIALS

Blue or khaki pigment-dyed hat (Pictured is Authentic Pigment brand in Indigo.)

Template (page 149)

Water-soluble marker

Tape

4-inch (10-cm) plastic embroidery hoop

Size 18 chenille needle

Embroidery scissors

EMBROIDERY THREAD COLORS

Light green (DMC 471)

Dark green (DMC 895)

White (DMC 3865)

Medium red (DMC 347)

Light red (DMC 350)

Indigo (DMC 333)

Medium yellow (DMC 725)

Light blue (DMC 157) (optional)

01.

02.

03.

04.

EMBROIDER!

01. Transfer the pattern onto the hat using the method from the beginning of the chapter (page 18). This entire project will be created using the Double Thread Method (page 9). Place the pattern closer to the front of the hat so the fern can take up a whole panel, rather than stitching it on a seam.

02. Stitch the stem of the fern with your light green embroidery thread. Start at the base of the stem and use the backstitch (page 11). Create the tip of the fern using a fishbone stitch (page 13).

03. Use single stitches at an angle to create the remainder of the fern leaves. As you go further down the plant, the leaves will get longer.

04. Switch to the dark green thread and, using the backstitch, create the stems for the Indian paintbrush and the lily of the valley. Using the white thread, create the lily of the valley flowers with the floral bud stitch (page 13).

05.

06.

07.

05. Create the Indian paintbrush flowers by using the medium red and light red threads in single stitches at the end of the green stems. Stitch the top of the Indian paintbrush with light red thread in a floral bud stitch. Create the small red buds in the design with the medium red thread using the floral bud stitch.

06. Create the daisy flowers using the daisy shape method (page 12) with the indigo thread and the medium yellow thread for the pollen.

07. You are done stitching the pattern, but you can keep going! Add small floral buds in light blue, light green and medium yellow in the empty spaces of the design. Add as many or as few as you'd like in varying sizes. I love using these filler flowers to make the design feel full and colorful. Remove the hoop to add flowers below the design.

08. Remove the water-soluble marker lines, as described on page 19. Your hat is ready to be worn!

Colorful and Creative
BANDANAS

Bandanas! These embroidered cuties can be used for so many things—from a scarf or headband to a handbag accent or puppy accessory. In this chapter you will learn how to make these inexpensive fabric squares unique and gorgeous by adding hand embroidery. Never use a plain bandana again when you can always add a chic touch quickly and with ease! Carry spring around with you every day with these happy blooms.

The patterns are designed to be stitched on the corners of cotton fabric, and you can also use them for various other projects! Tea towels, napkins and tablecloths would all look lovely with the addition of these colorful stitches. As long as light can easily pass through the fabric, you're good to go!

Get ready to explore the tropics with birds-of-paradise (page 83), get decked out in daisies (page 65) and take a trip to an Italian countryside filled with red poppies (page 75). Let's get stitching!

TIPS FOR CHOOSING A BANDANA

These days, bandanas come in a plethora of patterns and colors, so I encourage you to find the colors that make you happiest. I chose plain cotton bandanas to demonstrate the embroidery patterns; you can easily find them on Amazon or at your local craft store. The patterns would look beautiful on paisley bandanas as well! If you go with paisley, I recommend selecting light colors, such as white or red, so you can easily transfer the design onto the fabric.

ATTACHING AN EMBROIDERY HOOP TO A BANDANA

You will use an embroidery hoop for every project in this chapter. In the step-by-step images, the bandanas are displayed without a hoop; that is to fully present the embroidery technique for each project step. Using a hoop will yield the best results.

First, separate the hoop into two pieces, the inner ring and the outer ring. The outer ring has a metal screw on top that can tighten or loosen the hoop.

Begin with the bandana lying flat. Place the inner hoop on the back side of the bandana. Determine which side is the back of the bandana by looking at the seam along the edge of the fabric: the back side is where the seam's edge overlaps. Make sure the inner hoop is fully under the fabric. Place the outer hoop on top of the bandana and match it up with the inner hoop. Push until the two lock into place. If the fabric is not fully within the hoop, remove the outer hoop and try again. Pull the fabric tight to create a flat surface inside the hoop and tighten the metal screw.

You may need to stitch without the hoop to reach parts of the fabric that the hoop normally overlaps. For example, when adding the colorful floral bud stitches at the end of each design just hold the fabric taut as you go, avoiding wrinkles and bunching as much as you can.

BANDANA PATTERN TRANSFER TUTORIAL

01. Cut out the designated template from the back of the book.

02. Lay the bandana face down. Place the paper cutout face down on the corner of your bandana and use tape to secure it.

03. Flip the bandana over. It should be easy to see the design through the fabric. If you need to, shine a flashlight or cell phone light behind the pattern. Trace the lines with your water-soluble marker.

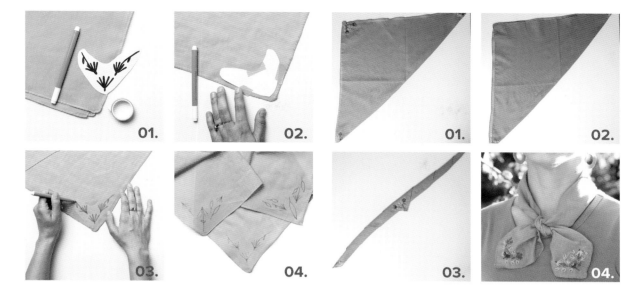

04. Continue transferring patterns to the other corners of the bandana. Now attach your hoop according to my instructions and embroider!

05. Once you are done, remove the blue lines using a cotton swab dipped in water. Blot the lines and watch them disappear. If the ink does not disappear, submerge the spot in water.

BANDANA EMBROIDERY TIPS

Be sure to tie off your thread between floral elements. Do not cross between floral elements; the threads will show up as lines through the fabric.

Tug the fabric tight as you stitch to avoid wrinkles and bunching. Tug the end, the corner and the edges of the fabric on the left and right side of the hoop regularly to maintain a flat stitching surface.

In the projects that follow, designs are given for three of the bandana corners. Feel free to embroider the fourth corner if you'd like. I usually leave it blank because I style my bandanas as a neck scarf.

TO WEAR A BANDANA AS A NECK SCARF

01. Begin by folding the bandana in half, creating a triangle shape. Make sure all three triangle corners that you can see are embroidered.

02. Flip the bandana over so that the embroidered corner at the top of the triangle is face down.

03. Then, beginning at the wide end, fold the bandana over onto itself multiple times to create one long rectangular shape.

04. Wrap the bandana around your neck and secure it with a double knot. Adjust the ends to flare out, exhibiting the embroidery. The third corner should be visible at the back of your neck if the bandana is folded properly.

Daisy
DUDES

You're going to love learning this stitch. In an afternoon you can totally transform an accessory by creating a daisy garden. I made these daisies yellow because I like how they pop against the pink bandana, but try them in white, purple or any other color you like! This project is the perfect introduction to bandana embroidery. Because the design is simple, you get a chance to get comfortable working with the fabric and hoop placement. Always keep a flat surface to stitch on by pulling the fabric taut in the hoop, and don't be afraid to cut out a stitch and start over, if needed.

LEVEL: BEGINNER

MATERIALS

Light pink cotton bandana
Template (page 149)
Water-soluble marker
Tape
3-inch (7.5-cm) wooden embroidery hoop
Size 18 chenille needle
Embroidery scissors

EMBROIDERY THREAD COLORS

Medium green (DMC 905)
Medium yellow (DMC 725)
Medium orange (DMC 946)
Dark dusty pink (DMC 3350)

01.

02.

03.

04.

05.

EMBROIDER!

01. Transfer the pattern onto the three corners of the bandana, using the method from the beginning of the chapter (page 62). Use the Single Thread Method (page 8) for this project.

02. Begin corner 1 by stitching the daisy stems in your medium green thread, using the backstitch (page 11). Create the leaves by using a fishbone stitch (page 13).

03. Use the daisy shape method (page 12) to create the daisies in the medium yellow thread with medium orange thread for the pollen. If the daisy petals are longer than 1 single stitch, use the backstitch. Add various small buds in dark dusty pink and medium yellow using the floral bud stitch (page 13) to fill in the blank spaces.

04. Move on to corner 2 of the bandana and follow the same steps, beginning with the backstitch, followed by the daisy shape method and finishing with the floral bud stitch.

05. Stitch corner 3 of the bandana using the same methods. Embroider the fourth corner if you'd like; I usually leave it blank. I recommend stitching the pattern from corner 3 onto the fourth corner.

06. Remove the water-soluble marker lines, as described on page 19. Your bandana is ready to be worn!

Lovely
LAVENDER

This design is so playful. It's like a spring day! Much like daisies, lavender is an easy flower to stitch that adds so much to an accessory. Add a few sprigs and you suddenly have an extraordinary new addition to your closet. This project is a great example of designing with contrast in mind. The dark magenta in this pattern stands out when paired with the light purple and medium yellow, especially on a light fabric such as this white bandana. It makes the embroidery more eye-catching and dynamic.

LEVEL: BEGINNER

MATERIALS

White cotton bandana

Template (page 151)

Water-soluble marker

Tape

3-inch (7.5-cm) wooden embroidery hoop

Size 18 chenille needle

Embroidery scissors

EMBROIDERY THREAD COLORS

Medium green (DMC 905)

Light purple (DMC 554)

Light pink (DMC 761)

Medium yellow (DMC 725)

Dark dusty pink (DMC 3350)

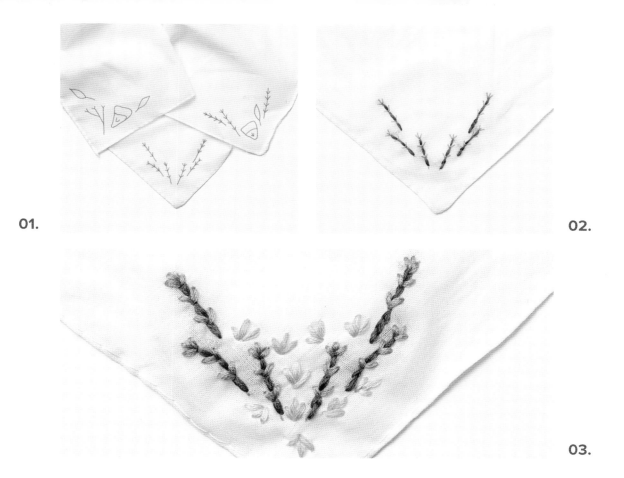

01.

02.

03.

EMBROIDER!

01. Transfer the pattern onto the bandana, using the method from the beginning of the chapter (page 62). This entire project will be created using the Double Thread Method (page 9).

02. Begin corner 1 by stitching the stems of the lavender with your medium green embroidery thread. Start at the base of the stems and use the backstitch (page 11).

03. Use the light purple thread to create floral buds (page 13) at the tip of each lavender stem. Continue adding flowers down the stem by using 2 stitches in a V shape for each flower. Add various small buds in light pink and medium yellow using the floral bud stitch to fill in the blank space around the lavender.

04.

05.

04. Move on to corner 2 and create the lavender stems. Stitch the leaf by using a fishbone stitch (page 13). The two-toned pink flowers are created by using the dark dusty pink and light pink threads with a long and short stitch (page 14). Begin with dark pink, creating a fan shape. Use the light pink to fill in the gaps and overlap the dark pink. Add pollen using the medium yellow thread to create 2 single stitches in a V shape. Stitch floral buds in yellow and light pink.

05. Create corner 3 of the bandana using the same methods. Embroider the fourth corner if you'd like. I usually leave it blank because of the way I like to style my bandanas. I recommend stitching the pattern from corner 1 onto the fourth corner.

06. Remove the water-soluble marker lines, as described on page 63. Your bandana is ready to be worn!

MUSHROOMS

I love embroidering little mushrooms! They are so easy to stitch and are great for folks who aren't super into flower motifs. When I look at this bandana, I think of a cute scarf accessory for a Girl Scout troop or a super useful head-band for a gardener getting their yard ready for spring. The design is great for bandanas, but it would also look cute on the corners of a tea towel! This pattern is a little more complex, so be mindful of the fabric bunching or wrinkling and keep it taut as you go. This design also includes greenery and white sprigs.

LEVEL: INTERMEDIATE

MATERIALS

Light blue cotton bandana

Template (page 153)

Water-soluble marker

Tape

3-inch (7.5-cm) wooden embroidery hoop

Size 18 chenille needle

Embroidery scissors

EMBROIDERY THREAD COLORS

Medium green (DMC 905)

White (DMC 3865)

Light brown (DMC 729)

Medium brown (DMC 301)

Medium red (DMC 349)

Light blue (DMC 747)

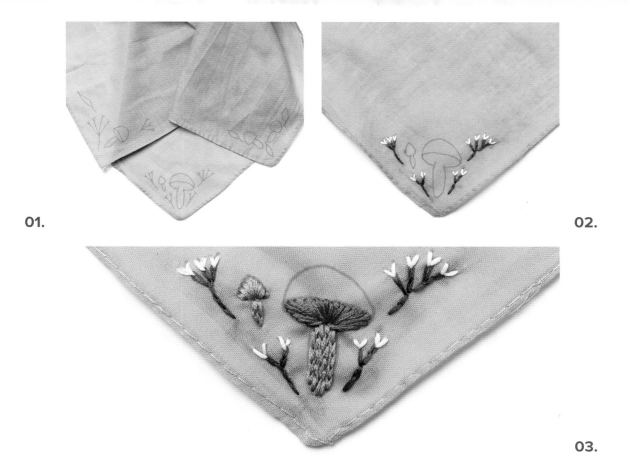

01.

02.

03.

EMBROIDER!

01. Transfer the pattern onto the bandana, using the method from the beginning of the chapter (page 62). This entire project will be created using the Single Thread Method (page 8).

02. Begin corner 1 by stitching the stems of the flowers with your medium green embroidery thread. Start at the base of the stems and use the backstitch (page 11). Create the flowers with the white thread using 2 single stitches in a V shape.

03. Using the light brown thread, create the mushroom stems with the backstitch. Stitch a few lines side by side until you have the desired stem width. Use the same thread with the satin stitch (page 14) to create the cap of the small mushroom. Switch to the medium brown thread to stitch the underside of the large mushroom's cap. Radiate the stitches in a fan shape from the tip of the stem.

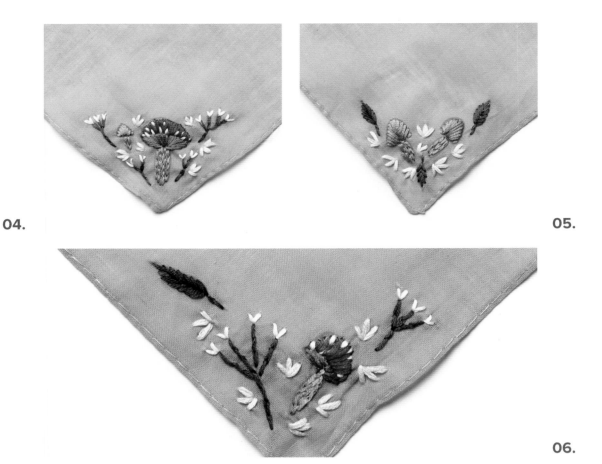

04.

05.

06.

04. Continue the larger mushroom with your medium red thread. Create the mushroom cap with the satin stitch and then switch to your white thread and add a few small single stitches in a random pattern, overlapping the red stitches. Stitch small buds in light blue using the floral bud stitch (page 13) to fill the blank space.

05. Move on to corner 2. Create the mushrooms using the light brown thread. Use the satin stitch for the mushroom caps and the backstitch in 3 lines for the stems. Create the leaves by using the medium green thread in a fishbone stitch (page 13).

06. Create corner 3 of the bandana using the same methods as corner 1. Embroider the fourth corner if you'd like; I usually leave it blank because of the way I like to style my bandanas. I recommend stitching the pattern from corner 1 onto the fourth corner.

07. Remove the water-soluble marker lines, as described on page 63. Your bandana is ready to be worn!

Red
POPPY PALS

When I traveled to Italy, my favorite place was a small village called Corciano. Along with being a lovely place surrounded by incredible olive trees and history, it was sprinkled with thousands of incredible red poppies. These flowers are striking and vibrant, which makes them the perfect addition to any embroidery pattern. They stand out on any fabric color. In this project, you will be using a simple color scheme. Not every embroidery design needs to use the entire rainbow. There can be beauty in using a few colors to create a complex and cohesive composition. This design also includes yellow daises and greenery.

LEVEL: INTERMEDIATE

MATERIALS

Light purple cotton bandana
Template (page 155)
Water-soluble marker
Tape
3-inch (7.5-cm) wooden embroidery hoop
Size 18 chenille needle
Embroidery scissors

EMBROIDERY THREAD COLORS

Medium green (DMC 905)
Medium yellow (DMC 725)
Dark red (DMC 815)
Medium red (DMC 349)
Dark brown (DMC 400)

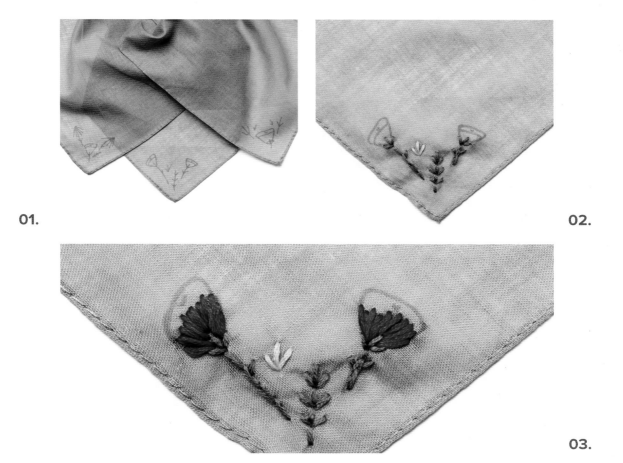

01.

02.

03.

EMBROIDER!

01. Transfer the pattern onto the bandana using the method from the beginning of the chapter (page 62). This entire project will be created using the Single Thread Method (page 8).

02. Begin corner 1 by stitching the stems with your medium green embroidery thread. Start at the base of the stems and use the backstitch (page 11). Create the leaves with single stitches. Stitch the tiny yellow bud with the medium yellow thread using the floral bud stitch (page 13).

03. The poppies are created using the long and short stitch (page 14). Use the dark red thread to stitch the bottoms of the poppy flowers, leaving space between the stitches.

04.

05.

06.

04. Switch to the medium red thread. Overlap the dark red stitches and fill in all gaps. Make the top of each flower a uniform line; do not leave a jagged edge with uneven stitches. Create the pollen with the medium yellow thread in a V shape. Stitch small floral buds in yellow to fill the blank space in the same style as the yellow bud in the design.

05. Move on to corner 2 and continue with the same methods. Begin with the backstitch for the stems, followed by the floral bud stitch for the small yellow flowers and the long and short stitch for the poppy. Create the leaves at the tip of each stem by using the medium green thread in a floral bud stitch.

06. Create corner 3 of the bandana using the same stitches and colors. The daisies are made using the daisy shape method (page 12) with the medium yellow thread for the petals and the dark brown thread for the pollen. Embroider the fourth corner if you'd like; I usually leave it blank because of the way I like to style my bandanas. I recommend stitching the pattern from corner 1 onto the fourth corner.

07. Remove the water-soluble marker lines, as described on page 63. Your bandana is ready to be worn!

 LEMON SLICES

This design is so spunky! It makes me think of enjoying the chilly comfort of a glass of fresh lemonade on a mercilessly hot summer day. I love stitching citrus of all types. I think they bring so much to a design that may otherwise feel a little two dimensional. Lemons are so satisfying to stitch because in no time, you go from a few basic shapes to a fruit that looks good enough to eat! This design also includes greenery and white sprigs.

LEVEL: ADVANCED

MATERIALS

Magenta cotton bandana

Template (page 157)

Water-soluble marker

Tape

3-inch (7.5-cm) wooden embroidery hoop

Size 18 chenille needle

Embroidery scissors

EMBROIDERY THREAD COLORS

Medium green (DMC 905)

White (DMC 3865)

Medium pink (DMC 760)

Medium yellow (DMC 725)

Light yellow (DMC 3822)

01.

02.

03.

EMBROIDER!

01. Transfer the pattern onto the bandana, using the method from the beginning of the chapter (page 62). This entire project will be created using the Single Thread Method (page 8).

02. Begin corner 1 by stitching the stems with your medium green embroidery thread. Start at the base of the stems and use the backstitch (page 11). Add the white flowers to the top of each stem by using 2 single stitches in a V shape. Stitch the floral buds with the medium pink thread using the floral bud stitch (page 13).

03. To create the lemon slice, begin with the medium yellow thread. Using the backstitch, outline the lemon peel in a curved shape. Switch to the white thread and continue with the backstitch to outline the inside of the lemon peel, the 4 inner lines and the outside edge of the fruit. Complete the slice by using the light yellow thread and the long and short stitch (page 14) to fill in the triangular shapes. Add more small pink floral buds to fill in the blank space.

04.

05.

04. Move on to corner 2 and continue with the same methods for the white floral sprig and floral buds. Use the fishbone stitch (page 13) to create the leaves. Create the tiny lemon by using the medium yellow thread with the satin stitch (page 14). Add in a few stitches of white thread to create a highlight effect on the upper right area of the lemon.

05. Create corner 3 of the bandana using the same methods as corner 1. Embroider the fourth corner if you'd like, I usually leave it blank because of the way I like to style my bandanas. I recommend stitching the pattern from corner 2 onto the fourth corner.

06. Remove the water-soluble marker lines, as described on page 63. Your bandana is ready to be worn!

Baby
BIRDS-OF-PARADISE

I love this tropical beauty! Some say birds-of-paradise flowers look like a bird in flight, while others think they look like the elegant neck and beak of a crane. I love stitching these flowers because the color scheme is one I would not have thought to use, but it works so well! That is one thing I love about embroidering flowers and plants; the shapes and colors found in nature can be so unexpected. I love challenging myself to re-create a plant that is especially out of my comfort zone and unlike anything I've created before. I have made this dynamic plant super easy to stitch in this inspiring tutorial. This design also includes greenery and red sprigs.

LEVEL: ADVANCED

MATERIALS

Yellow cotton bandana

Template (page 159)

Water-soluble marker

Tape

3-inch (7.5-cm) wooden embroidery hoop

Size 18 chenille needle

Embroidery scissors

EMBROIDERY THREAD COLORS

Dark teal (DMC 3847)

Medium red (DMC 349)

Light green (DMC 958)

Light orange (DMC 741)

Indigo (DMC 333)

01.

02.

03.

04.

05.

EMBROIDER!

01. Transfer the pattern onto the bandana, using the method from the beginning of the chapter (page 62). Use the Single Thread Method (page 8).

02. Begin corner 1 by stitching the stem of the bird-of-paradise with your dark teal thread, using the long and short stitch (page 14). Add a touch of red to the tip using the medium red thread with the backstitch (page 11). Stitch the leaves using the light green with a fishbone stitch (page 13).

03. To create the orange bird-of-paradise petals, use a fishbone stitch with the light orange thread. Switch to the indigo thread to outline the indigo petal using the backstitch. Add small floral buds (page 13) in red and indigo.

04. Repeat the same steps to create corner 2 of the bandana.

05. Begin corner 3 by stitching the stems with your light green embroidery thread, using the backstitch. Add the red flowers to each stem by using 2 to 3 single stitches per flower. Add orange and indigo floral buds. Embroider the fourth corner if you'd like; I usually leave it blank. I recommend stitching the pattern from corner 3 onto the fourth corner.

06. Remove the water-soluble marker lines, as described on page 63. Your bandana is ready to be worn!

Flowery
FANNY PACKS

Let me say that I am so happy fanny packs are back in style. They are functional and they come in so many cute colors and materials. I love taking something simple and useful and making it extra special by adding a customized touch with a beautiful embroidered design!

Stitched florals such as a gorgeous green monstera (page 93), lush lupine (page 91) and a radiant sunflower (page 97) are great for arts markets, travel days, music festivals, amusement parks and wherever else you'd like to be stylish and hands-free.

These patterns also look great on any small pouch, such as a makeup bag, pencil case or sewing supply kit.

TIPS FOR CHOOSING A FANNY PACK

I recommend going for a softer fabric for these projects, rather than your classic nylon fanny pack. In this book, I have used a cotton fanny pack that is super easy to embroider on. I find my fanny packs on Amazon by searching for "soft denim waist bag" or "cotton fanny pack." The fanny pack I use is 9 x 6.5 inches (23 x 16.5 cm) with a 4 x 9–inch (10 x 23–cm) stitching surface area. The stitching surface area is the front fabric of the fanny pack that is accessible through the front pouch.

ATTACHING AN EMBROIDERY HOOP TO A FANNY PACK

You will use an embroidery hoop for every project in this chapter. In some images, the fanny packs are displayed without a hoop; that is to fully present the embroidery technique for each project step. Using a hoop when it is called for will yield the best results.

Begin by separating the hoop into two pieces, the inner ring and the outer ring. The outer ring has a metal screw on top that can tighten or loosen the hoop.

Place the inner hoop on the inside of the fanny pack. Place the outer hoop on the outside of the fanny pack and match it up with the inner hoop. Push until the two lock into place. Pull the fabric tight on the inside of the hoop and tighten the metal screw. You may need to overlap the zipper, as shown in the photo, but that should be easy to do with the plastic hoop. You may need to pull hard to get a flat stitching surface; fanny packs are durable and will be fine.

FANNY PACK AND ZIPPER POUCH PATTERN TRANSFER TUTORIAL

A water-soluble stabilizer is a piece of material that allows you to temporarily affix a pattern to a piece of fabric for the purposes of sewing and embroidery. You can easily draw a design onto the stabilizer, peel off the back like a sticker and stick the stabilizer onto the fabric of your choice. This is super helpful for dark fabrics that do not work with the light box pattern transfer method. It is easy to stitch through the material of the stabilizer. When you're done embroidering, it washes away with water. In this book I use the Sulky Sticky Fabri-Solvy™ self-adhesive, fabric-like, water-soluble stabilizer.

01. Using scissors, cut out the pattern from the pattern template section.

02. Lay the water-soluble stabilizer sheet on top of the pattern cutout. You should be able to see the lines easily through the material. If it's hard to see, hold the pattern and stabilizer in front of a window or shine a flashlight underneath to illuminate the lines. Transfer the pattern onto the stabilizer sheet using a water-soluble marker. Use tape to keep the stabilizer still, if needed. Use scissors to cut the pattern out of the stabilizer sheet. Save the other half of the sheet for future projects.

03. Lay your fanny pack on a flat surface and make sure it is wrinkle-free. Peel the stabilizer off the paper backing and apply it carefully to the fabric. You're ready to stitch! You will be stitching directly through the stabilizer and the fabric.

04. Remove the stabilizer after the embroidery is complete. Run warm water over the design. Use your thumb to gently brush away the visible stabilizer material. It will peel away as the water soaks into it. Blow-dry or air-dry your fanny pack.

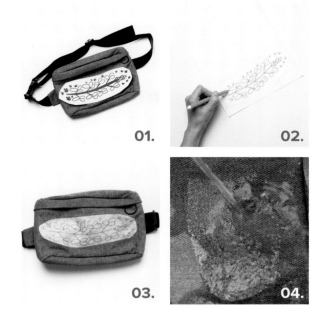

01. 02.

03. 04.

FANNY PACK EMBROIDERY TIPS

If the chenille needle is hard to get through the fabric, use a thimble or rubber finger grip.

Sewing inside of a small space is a little challenging. Don't be afraid to take the hoop off the fanny pack sometimes, if needed, to make more room for your hand.

The more you stitch, the more secure your stabilizer will be. In these patterns, I put the small buds and flowers early in the tutorial, so the perimeter of the stabilizer is stitched to the fabric. If the stabilizer unsticks, just press it down lightly.

Keep adding elements! Add more daisies and floral buds if you'd like. Make it yours!

Lush
LUPINE

Wildflowers are the perfect addition to any accessory. Adding something timelessly resplendent such as a lupine makes this on-trend fanny pack wearable for life. This fanny pack is the perfect place to stow away your wallet and a snack during a morning hike. In this project, you will get great practice working in a small space. Try to open up the zipper of the bag as much as you can, holding the bag open with your non-dominant hand as you stitch with the other. Switch up the colors of the little buds or add more—make it your own!

LEVEL: BEGINNER

MATERIALS

Light wash denim or light blue cotton fanny pack

Template (page 159)

Self-adhesive, fabric-like, water-soluble stabilizer (My favorite is the Sulky Sticky Fabri-Solvy brand.)

Water-soluble marker

Tape

4-inch (10-cm) plastic embroidery hoop

Size 18 chenille needle

Embroidery scissors

EMBROIDERY THREAD COLORS

Dark hunter green (DMC 3345)

Dark dusty pink (DMC 3350)

Light yellow (DMC 743)

Dark blue (DMC 820)

Indigo (DMC 333)

Light purple (DMC 211)

White (DMC 3865)

Light green (DMC 471)

01.

02.

03.

04.

EMBROIDER!

01. Transfer the pattern onto the fanny pack, using the method from the beginning of the chapter (page 88). This entire project will be created using the Double Thread Method (page 9).

02. Stitch the stem with your dark hunter green embroidery floss. Start at the base of the stem and use the backstitch (page 11). Create the tip of the lupine using the fishbone stitch (page 13). The small flower buds are created with 3 single stitches in a floral bud stitch (page 13) with the dark dusty pink and light yellow threads.

03. Using the satin stitch (page 14), fill in each lupine flower shape with stitches angled in toward the stem. Create a beautiful gradient effect by beginning with dark blue at the base, followed by indigo and light purple.

04. Add 2 white stitches to the center of each lupine flower. Add light green and white stitches to the tip of the stem, overlapping the hunter green thread.

05. Remove the stabilizer, as described on page 89. Your fanny pack is ready to be worn!

Tropical
MONSTERA

These gorgeous houseplants have taken the world by storm! And rightly so, because their giant, lush leaves are absolutely awe-inspiring. Also known as the Swiss cheese plant, *Monstera deliciosa* is a tropical plant that can be found growing in the wild or living in a pot in your home. This project is a great way to practice color blending with thread to create dimension and light. Many artists describe embroidery as painting with thread, and using the long and short stitch in this pattern is the perfect example of that. I love how the vivid greens of the leaf complement the denim tone of this fanny pack. This design would also be stunning on a denim jacket or pair of jeans!

LEVEL: INTERMEDIATE

MATERIALS

Light wash denim or light blue cotton fanny pack

Template (page 161)

Self-adhesive, fabric-like, water-soluble stabilizer (My favorite is the Sulky Sticky Fabri-Solvy brand.)

Water-soluble marker

Tape

4-inch (10-cm) plastic embroidery hoop

Size 18 chenille needle

Embroidery scissors

EMBROIDERY THREAD COLORS

Dark dusty pink (DMC 3350)

Medium orange (DMC 946)

Medium yellow (DMC 725)

Dark emerald green (DMC 909)

Medium green (DMC 702)

Dark green (DMC 890)

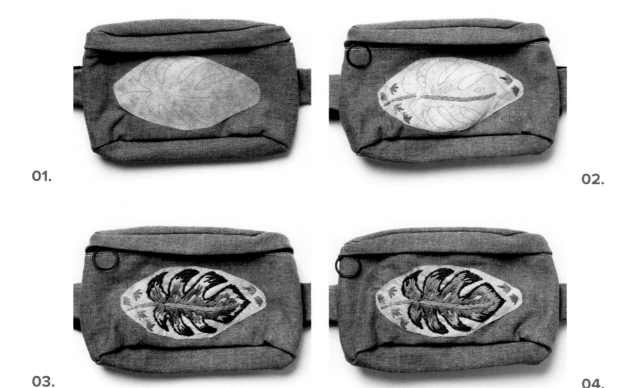

01.

02.

03.

04.

EMBROIDER!

01. Transfer the pattern onto the fanny pack, using the method from the beginning of the chapter (page 88). This entire project uses the Double Thread Method (page 9).

02. Stitch the flowers using the daisy shape method (page 12) and medium yellow thread for the pollen. Begin with the dark dusty pink flowers, followed by the medium orange flowers, using dark emerald green thread for the stems. Create the Monstera stem with your medium green thread, using the backstitch (page 11). Start at the base and use 2 to 3 lines side by side for the appropriate width.

03. Continue the leaf with the dark emerald green thread using the long and short stitch (page 14). Begin the stitches next to the stem and stitch about one-third of the way down each shape using stitches in alternating lengths. Switch to the dark green thread and use the long and short stitch and backstitch to fill in the ends and outside edge of the leaf. Leave a small gap between the dark green and dark emerald threads.

04. Use the medium green thread with the long and short stitch to fill in the gap, creating a highlight effect.

05. Remove the stabilizer, as described on page 89. Your fanny pack is ready to be worn!

Radiant
SUNFLOWER

I love stitching sunflowers! They are definitely in my top five favorite flowers to add to an accessory for the ultimate vibrant pop. They remind me of summer gardens and dazzling wedding bouquets. There are lots of different ways to create flower petals, as seen in this book, but for sunflowers I always choose the fishbone stitch. Although it is typically used for leaves, I love how uniform it is. It's perfect for creating petals on a symmetrical flower, such as a sunflower. If you're feeling extra inspired, you can stitch multiple sunflowers onto one fanny pack, making it a full-on garden! This design also includes colorful daisies and floral sprigs.

LEVEL: ADVANCED

MATERIALS

Light wash denim or light blue cotton fanny pack

Template (page 161)

Self-adhesive, fabric-like, water-soluble stabilizer (My favorite is the Sulky Sticky Fabri-Solvy brand.)

Water-soluble marker

Tape

4-inch (10-cm) plastic embroidery hoop

Size 18 chenille needle

Embroidery scissors

EMBROIDERY THREAD COLORS

Medium green (DMC 702)

Light purple (DMC 554)

Dark dusty pink (DMC 3350)

Medium yellow (DMC 725)

Medium orange (DMC 946)

Dark hunter green (DMC 3345)

Dark brown (DMC 300)

Medium brown (DMC 301)

01.

02.

EMBROIDER!

01. Transfer the pattern onto the fanny pack, using the method from the beginning of the chapter (page 88). This entire project will be created using the Double Thread Method (page 9).

02. Begin with the small floral elements and leaves. Use the medium green thread and create the stems using the backstitch (page 11), starting at the base of the stems. Use the daisy shape method (page 12) to create the daisies in light purple and dark dusty pink, with medium yellow thread for the pollen. Add 2 single stitches at the top of each flower bud stem in a V shape using the medium orange thread to create the small buds. Create the dark hunter green leaves using the fishbone stitch (page 13).

03.

04.

03. Stitch the center circle of the sunflower with your dark brown embroidery thread using the satin stitch (page 14). Switch to the medium brown thread and continuing with the satin stitch, create the outer circle radiating out from the inner circle like rays of sunshine.

04. The petals of the sunflower are created using the fishbone stitch with your medium yellow thread.

05. Remove the stabilizer, as described on page 89. Your fanny pack is ready to be worn!

Too Cute TOTE BAGS

I absolutely love these totes! It is so rewarding to add your own creative touch to something you can show off every day. Adding embroidery is a quick and easy way to customize your otherwise ordinary tote bags. If you have been looking to decrease your carbon footprint and reduce your plastic bag waste, reusable totes are the perfect stylish addition on your path to a green life! Buy a plain tote to decorate or add some stitched sass to one that is already in your collection.

I love bringing these with me to my local Saturday farmers' market to fill up with locally grown goodies, local bread and pesto. Yum!

Enjoy personalizing your very own go-to bag with a gorgeous coffee plant (page 105), succulent buddies (page 113) and a fruit medley (page 109)!

The patterns are designed to be stitched onto cotton fabric, and you can also use them for various other projects. Pillowcases, aprons, tea towels and linen blouses would all look beautiful with the addition of these colorful stitches. As long as light can easily pass through the fabric, you're good to go!

TIPS FOR CHOOSING A TOTE BAG

The tote bags I use in this book are 15 x 16–inch (38 x 40.5–cm) cotton totes in the color "natural"; they are easy to find at craft stores or on Amazon. A smaller tote bag would be suitable as well. I recommend using a tote bag in a light color to help you easily transfer the pattern onto the fabric.

ATTACHING AN EMBROIDERY HOOP TO A TOTE BAG

You will use an embroidery hoop for every project in this chapter.

Begin by separating the hoop into two pieces, the inner ring and the outer ring. The outer ring has a metal screw on top that can tighten or loosen the hoop.

Lay the tote bag on a flat surface. Place the inner hoop on the inside of the tote bag and position it in the center of the fabric. Place the outer hoop on the outside of the tote bag and match it up with the inner hoop. Push until the two lock into place. Pull the fabric tight on the inside of the hoop and tighten the metal screw.

TOTE BAG PATTERN TRANSFER TUTORIAL

01. Cut out the designated pattern from the back of the book. Apply the hoop to your tote bag.

02. Turn the tote bag inside out and place the paper cutout face down inside your hoop. When the pattern is in the desired spot, use tape to temporarily adhere it to the tote fabric.

03. Flip the tote bag back to its normal orientation. Use a bright window or cell phone flashlight to illuminate the design from behind for better visibility. Transfer your pattern using a water-soluble marker. It's okay if you make mistakes; you will remove leftover marks at the end. It will be easiest to see the lines if the paper is pressed firmly against the fabric.

04. Remove the paper from the inside of the tote bag and begin stitching!

05. To remove the lines after embroidering, use a cotton swab dipped in water and blot the visible blue lines. If the ink does not disappear immediately, submerge the spot in water and let the tote bag air-dry.

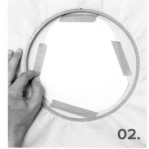

TOTE BAG EMBROIDERY TIPS

I recommend cutting and tying off the thread between each floral element so there isn't any thread crossover between flowers. It's important to keep your stitches tidy when stitching on a surface that is light colored and may be see-through.

Have an iron or steamer on hand to remove the wrinkles left by the embroidery hoop.

 Sprouting
COFFEE PLANT

Coffee has such a nostalgic scent for me. It reminds me of my grandparents, who always offer to put on a pot of coffee when they have company over, no matter the time of the day. So many people love the taste, the pick-me-up and the culture of coffee. Despite it being so well loved, a lot of avid coffee drinkers haven't seen the coffee plant that their favorite brew comes from. This design is the perfect crossover gift for a coffee drinker and plant lover—I expect you know a few. It shows the coffee plant stalk with cute red coffee cherries and small flower buds. In this project, you will be creating leaves in a whole new way. Rather than using the fishbone stitch, you will be using the satin stitch in two colors to create dimension in the leaves.

LEVEL: BEGINNER

MATERIALS

Natural or khaki cotton tote bag

Template (page 163)

Water-soluble marker

Tape

8-inch (20-cm) wooden embroidery hoop

Size 18 chenille needle

Embroidery scissors

EMBROIDERY THREAD COLORS

Dark hunter green (DMC 3345)

Light green (DMC 988)

Dark green (DMC 890)

Red (DMC 816)

White (DMC 3865)

Indigo (DMC 333)

Light pink (DMC 352)

Light orange (DMC 3853)

Medium yellow (DMC 725)

01.

02.

03.

EMBROIDER!

01. Transfer the pattern onto the tote bag, using the method from the beginning of the chapter (page 103). This entire project will be created using the Double Thread Method (page 9).

02. Begin by stitching the stem starting at the base, using the dark hunter green thread and the backstitch (page 11). Create the line in the center of each leaf with the same stitch. Stitch the small leaves at the tip of the plant with the fishbone stitch (page 13).

03. The leaves of the coffee plant are created using the satin stitch (page 14). Begin with your light green thread and fill in the top half of each leaf using the satin stitch. The stitches should run perpendicular to the line that intersects each leaf.

04.

05.

04. Switch to the dark green thread and continue the same method on the underside of the leaves. Create the coffee cherries with the satin stitch and red thread. Add a small white stitch to each berry to create a highlight effect. Continue with the white thread to create the small flowers, which are made of 4 to 5 single stitches.

05. Use the indigo, light pink, light orange and medium yellow threads to add the small flowers. Some of the small flowers are made using the floral bud stitch (page 13). The others are daisies, created using the daisy shape method (page 12) with orange and yellow single stitches for the pollen.

06. Remove the water-soluble marker lines, as described on page 103. I ironed my tote bag at the end to remove the crease from the hoop.

Fresh
FRUIT

This design looks absolutely delicious! The colorful fruit medley consists of lemons, strawberries and kiwis, plus lots of vibrant daisies, floral sprigs and a lil' bleeding-heart. I love the challenge of branching out from flowers and stitching fruits and vegetables, finding inspiration in botanical illustrations, paintings and vintage embroidered pieces depicting these sweet shapes. In this project, your embroidery skills will be taken to a whole new level! You'll master the long and short stitch as you create your first kiwis! Add more colorful floral buds to this design at the end to make it a rainbow, if you'd like!

LEVEL: INTERMEDIATE

MATERIALS

Natural or khaki cotton tote bag

Template (page 165)

Water-soluble marker

Tape

8-inch (20-cm) wooden embroidery hoop

Size 18 chenille needle

Embroidery scissors

EMBROIDERY THREAD COLORS

Medium green (DMC 905)

Light green (DMC 906)

Dark green (DMC 890)

Dark dusty pink (DMC 3350)

Medium purple (DMC 552)

Medium yellow (DMC 725)

White (DMC 3865)

Light yellow (DMC 3822)

Light red (DMC 666)

Dark brown (DMC 400)

Lime green (DMC 907)

Light orange (DMC 741)

Light pink (DMC 761)

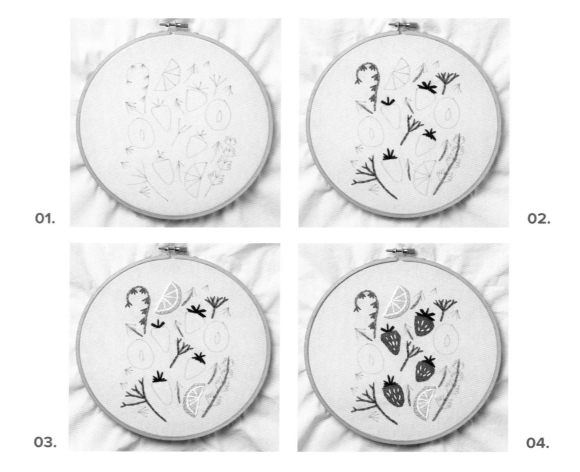

01.

02.

03.

04.

EMBROIDER!

01. Transfer the pattern onto the tote bag using the method from the beginning of the chapter (page 103). This entire project will be created using the Double Thread Method (page 9).

02. Begin by stitching the stems using the medium green and light green threads. Start at the base of the stems and use the backstitch (page 11). Use the dark green thread in 5 to 10 single stitches to create the strawberry stems. Use the floral bud stitch (page 13) with the dark dusty pink thread to create the bleeding-heart flowers. Add 2 single stitches to the top of each stem in a V shape to create the purple sprigs, using the medium purple thread.

03. To create the lemon slices, begin with the medium yellow thread. Using the backstitch, outline the lemon peel in a curved shape with 2 lines side by side. Switch to the white thread and continue with the backstitch to outline the inside of the lemon peel, the 4 white lines and the outside edge of the fruit. Complete the slice by using the light yellow thread and the long and short stitch (page 14) to fill in the triangular shapes.

04. Outline the strawberries using the backstitch with the light red thread. Fill the inside of the strawberries using the same color with the long and short stitch. Add single stitches in white thread to create the strawberry seeds.

05.

06.

07.

05. Create the kiwis by beginning with the dark brown thread. Use the backstitch to outline each kiwi shape. Stitch an oval in white in the center of the kiwi using the satin stitch (page 14). Switch to the lime green and use the long and short stitch to create stitches radiating out from the white oval.

06. Continue the kiwi by adding in light green thread with the long and short stitch, overlapping and filling between the lime green stitches. The seeds are created using the brown thread in a few short single stitches.

07. The dark dusty pink, orange and light pink daisies are created using the daisy shape method (page 12) with medium yellow thread for the pollen. The snapdragon is created using the dark dusty pink and light pink threads, filling in each shape with the satin stitch.

08. Remove the water-soluble marker lines, as described on page 103. I ironed my tote bag at the end to remove the crease from the hoop.

Colorful
SUCCULENTS

Succulents!!! These little dudes are trickier to keep alive than you may think. Too much water, too little water: the balance can seem like a mystery. But you know what kind of succulent you can't tragically over-water? An embroidered one. I love this spunky design with three happy succulents in earthy tones! It's perfect to stitch onto a tote for all of your plant shopping needs. There's no such thing as too many plants. This is one of my favorite designs in this book. I love how layering the thread colors and adding a highlight color can add so much depth to a two-dimensional work of art. Have fun with this design, and feel free to add more small flowers once the design is complete.

LEVEL: ADVANCED

MATERIALS

Natural or khaki cotton tote bag
Template (page 167)
Water-soluble marker
Tape
8-inch (20-cm) wooden embroidery hoop
Size 18 chenille needle
Embroidery scissors

EMBROIDERY THREAD COLORS

Dark hunter green (DMC 3345)
Medium purple (DMC 3835)
Medium green (DMC 702)
Light green (DMC 471)
Light pink (DMC 761)
Medium pink (DMC 223)
Light purple (DMC 211)

01.

02.

03

EMBROIDER!

01. Transfer the pattern onto the tote bag, using the method from the beginning of the chapter (page 103). This entire project will be created using the Double Thread Method (page 9).

02. Begin by stitching the stems using the dark hunter green thread. Start at the base of each stem and use the backstitch (page 11). Create the leaves by using the satin stitch (page 14) in the same color.

03. To create each succulent, begin with the outline color. Start with the top succulent, which has a medium purple outline and a medium green and light green interior. Use single stitches and the backstitch to outline the succulent. Switch to the medium green thread and, with the long and short stitch (page 14), begin to fill in the inside of each succulent leaf.

04.

05.

06.

04. Switch to the light green thread and use the long and short stitch to complete the top half of each succulent leaf, being careful not to overlap the purple outline. Feel free to overlap the medium green stitches.

05. Use the same method with the other succulents. The big green succulent uses light green for the outline with dark hunter green and medium green for the leaves. The pink succulent is created using light pink for the outline with medium pink for the inside of the leaves.

06. Use medium pink and light purple to create the small floral buds (page 13). Use the light purple thread to outline the tip of each leaf of the purple succulent with the backstitch. Do the same to the green succulent with the light pink thread.

07. Remove the water-soluble marker lines, as described on page 103. I ironed my tote bag at the end to remove the crease from the hoop.

A Garden of
FLORAL PATCHES

Patches are a super fun way to decorate accessories, especially ones that may be a little tricky to embroider on directly. Adhere them to backpacks, denim jackets, jeans, flannels and hats—the options are endless. They are a wonderful gift for an embroidery-loving friend, allowing them to choose their own adventure and attach the patch to whatever their heart desires!

Any of the patterns in this book can be used as a patch, but I made these three especially for this chapter. Get lost in a snapdragon rainbow (page 123), get your macramé fix with a pothos pattern (page 125) and finish up with adorable pansy pals (page 129).

These designs can be embroidered directly onto anything you'd like! Think linen clothing, aprons, tote bags or pillowcases. As long as light can pass through the fabric, you're good to go!

TIPS FOR CHOOSING PATCH FABRIC

When choosing your patch fabric, I recommend cotton or a linen/cotton blend. Choose a fabric in any color as long as you can still see through it. You need it to be see-through to trace the pattern using the lightbox method.

The fabric should be cut into a square that is approximately 3 inches (7.5 cm) wider and longer than the embroidery hoop.

ATTACHING AN EMBROIDERY HOOP TO PATCH FABRIC

You will use an embroidery hoop for every project in this chapter.

Begin by separating the hoop into two pieces, the inner ring and the outer ring. The outer ring has a metal screw on top that can tighten or loosen the hoop.

Begin with the fabric lying flat. Place the inner hoop underneath the fabric. Place the outer hoop on top of the fabric and match it up with the inner hoop. Push until the two lock into place. Pull the fabric tight to create a flat surface inside the hoop and tighten the metal screw.

EMBROIDERED PATCH PATTERN TUTORIAL

01. Cut out the designated pattern from the back of the book. Apply the hoop to your patch fabric.

02. Flip the hoop over and place the paper cutout face down inside your hoop. When the pattern is in the desired spot, use tape to temporarily adhere it to the fabric.

03. Turn the hoop over and trace the lines with a water-soluble marker. Use a bright window or cell phone light to illuminate the design from behind for better visibility. It's okay if you make mistakes; you will remove leftover marks at the end. It will be easiest to see the lines if the paper is pressed firmly against the fabric.

01. Cut the patch out in the shape of your choice (e.g., circle, square or the same shape as the design) with about ½ inch (1.3 cm) of space between the embroidery and the edge of the fabric.

04. Remove the paper from the inside of the hoop and begin stitching!

05. To remove the lines after embroidering, use a cotton swab dipped in water and blot the visible blue lines. If the ink does not disappear immediately, submerge the spot in water and let it air-dry.

02. Pin the patch to your surface or use your thumb and index finger to hold the patch in place. In the color of your choosing, sew around the edge of the patch using the whipstitch (page 15), creating a stitch every few millimeters until the patch is fully attached.

ATTACHING PATCHES

There are two different methods for affixing a patch to clothing or accessories.

Sew-On Method: I recommend this method for small patches. It is quick and easy to attach a patch to your favorite vest or jacket. All you need is embroidery thread and you're ready to get started!

Iron-On Method: I recommend this for medium to large patches. Ironing on a patch allows the full patch to lay flat on whatever surface you attach it to. If you sew larger patches on, they may appear loose and wrinkled.

For this process, I use a double-sided, heat-activated bonding material. I prefer HeatnBond Ultrahold. This will permanently affix your patch to whatever surface you choose, making sure it lasts through wear and washes. You can find this on Amazon or at any craft store.

Rather than attaching the adhesive directly to the back of your embroidery design, I recommend adding a fabric backing. A fabric backing supports the fabric, helping it retain its shape and flatness, and it serves as a surface for the adhesive to properly stick to. I like to use felt as my fabric backing because it is more rigid than cotton and helps the patch keep its shape. A piece of cotton fabric will also work; just be sure it is ironed flat.

01.

01. Cut the patch out in the shape of your choice (e.g., circle, square or the same shape as the design) with about ½ inch (1.3 cm) of space between the embroidery and the edge of the fabric. Cut out a piece of felt or a second piece of cotton fabric in the same size.

02.

02. Use embroidery thread to attach the two fabrics using the whipstitch (page 15) with the stitches close together.

03.   04.

03. Finish the stitch in the back of the design so the knot is hidden.

04. Cut out the iron-on adhesive; I prefer HeatnBond Ultrahold. Use an iron to bond it to the back of your design.

05. Peel off the paper liner. Place your patch onto the desired location and iron it on for the recommended amount of time. I suggest ironing the patch on from the inside of the fabric, as it will activate the adhesive more quickly.

PATCH EMBROIDERY TIPS

I recommend cutting and tying off the thread between each floral element so there isn't any thread crossover between flowers. It's important to keep your stitches tidy when stitching on a surface that is light colored and may be see-through.

Keep the thread tight by regularly tugging at the edges around the hoop to be sure there is a flat surface to stitch on.

snapdragon
RAINBOW

I am a sucker for snapdragons! Stick them in a bouquet or a flower arrangement and I'm sold. These colorful pals are easy to stitch. Add this patch to a jacket, backpack or anything denim. This design would be a great addition to tea towels, right along the bottom edge. Personalize this pattern by adding small floral buds in a rainbow of colors or by stitching some text below it using the backstitch. Play with the color combination on these snapdragons; they come in so many vibrant tones from bright red to deep magenta. I suggest using the sew-on method to attach this patch to a surface.

LEVEL: BEGINNER

MATERIALS

Your choice of cotton fabric

Template (page 169)

Water-soluble marker

Tape

6-inch (15-cm) embroidery hoop

Size 18 chenille needle

Embroidery scissors

EMBROIDERY THREAD COLORS

Dark hunter green (DMC 3345)

Light orange (DMC 3853)

Light yellow (DM 3822)

Medium purple (DMC 552)

Medium yellow (DMC 725)

Medium pink (DMC 602)

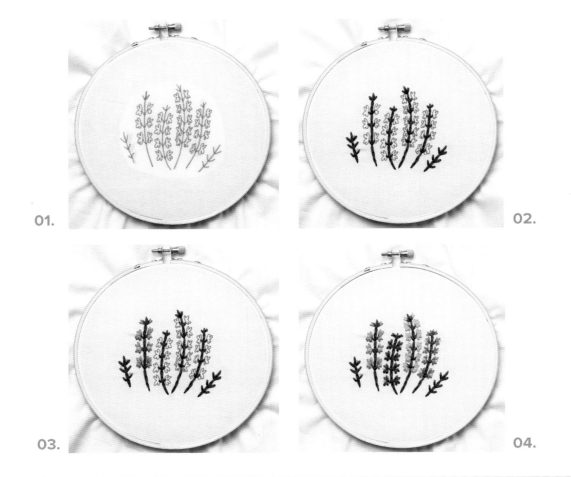

01.

02.

03.

04.

EMBROIDER!

01. Transfer the pattern onto the fabric using the method from the beginning of the chapter (page 118). This entire project will be created using the Double Thread Method (page 9).

02. Stitch the stems with your dark hunter green embroidery thread. Start at the base of the stems and use the backstitch (page 11). Create the leaves using single stitches.

03. Each snapdragon is made up of the primary color and the light yellow accent. Start with the light orange snapdragon. Using single stitches, fill in each flower petal with approximately 2 to 4 stitches toward the stem. Add the yellow accent to the center of each petal shape using a single stitch.

04. Continue stitching the rest of the colors in order: medium purple, medium yellow and medium pink.

05. Remove the water-soluble marker lines and attach the patch, using the sew-on method, to your desired surface, as described on page 119.

Overflowing
POTHOS PLANTER

When I started embroidery, I was also playing around with macramé. One of the first things I created was a macramé plant hanger. It was quick, surprisingly easy and—best of all—it was useful! These days, my husband Jesse is the plant wrangler in our household. We have a room in our home dedicated to our green friends that we lovingly call the Plant Room. It houses many of my macramé plant hangers, from easy knots to advanced designs. My favorite plant to stick in a hanging planter is golden pothos, which is why I wanted to share this patch with you. This lovable houseplant is extra easy to keep alive and grows long tendrils that can reach the floor with enough time and love!

LEVEL: INTERMEDIATE

MATERIALS

Your choice of cotton fabric

Template (page 169)

Water-soluble marker

Tape

6-inch (15-cm) embroidery hoop

Size 18 chenille needle

Embroidery scissors

Felt (optional)

Iron-on adhesive

EMBROIDERY THREAD COLORS

Medium green (DMC 905)

Light green (DMC 988)

Medium yellow (DMC 725)

Dark orange (DMC 900)

Light orange (DMC 3853)

White (DMC 3865)

Medium purple (DMC 552)

Medium blue (DMC 3760)

01. 02. 03.

04. 05.

EMBROIDER!

01. Transfer the pattern onto the fabric using the method from the beginning of the chapter (page 118). This project uses the Double Thread Method (page 9).

02. Start at the base of the pothos stems with your medium green thread, using the backstitch (page 11). Create the leaves with 1 to 2 single stitches. Use the light green thread for the daisy stems.

03. Add a line of the medium yellow thread to a few leaves to create the variegated color that golden pothos are known for.

04. Outline the pot in the dark orange thread using the backstitch. Fill in the pot with the light orange thread using the satin stitch (page 14). I like to do my satin stitch horizontally for flowerpots.

05. Use the white thread and the backstitch to create the macramé rope. Use the satin stitch to create the knots in the rope. Add the floral buds (page 13) using 3 to 5 stitches in medium purple and medium blue. Create the daises using the daisy shape method (page 12) in blue and yellow. For the blue flowers, use yellow thread for the pollen; for the yellow flowers, use the light orange thread.

06. Remove the water-soluble marker lines and attach the patch, using the iron-on method, to your desired surface, as described on page 119.

Pansy
PALS

Pansies are such a nostalgic flower for so many of the people I've stitched for. They remind me of childhood stories, especially Lewis Carroll's *Alice's Adventures in Wonderland*. They can't help but look like little faces! This elegant, timeless patch would look so gorgeous on the back of a jacket, the top compartment of a backpack or on a handmade quilt. I recommend keeping your stitches uniform and clean while working on this design. Enjoy creating this modern twist on a classic motif!

LEVEL: ADVANCED

MATERIALS

Your choice of cotton fabric
Template (page 169)
Water-soluble marker
Tape
6-inch (15-cm) embroidery hoop
Size 18 chenille needle
Embroidery scissors
Felt (optional)
Iron-on adhesive

EMBROIDERY THREAD COLORS

Light green (DMC 470)
Light orange (DMC 3853)
Light pink (DMC 761)
Indigo (DMC 333)
Light yellow (DMC 727)
Medium blue (DMC 3891)
Light blue (DMC 3845)
Medium yellow (DMC 725)
Medium red (DMC 349)
Light red (DMC 350)
Medium purple (DMC 552)
Light purple (DMC 211)

01.

02.

03.

EMBROIDER!

01. Transfer the pattern onto the fabric using the method from the beginning of the chapter (page 118). This entire project will be created using the Double Thread Method (page 9).

02. Stitch the stems with your light green embroidery thread. Start at the base of the stems and use the backstitch (page 11). Create the leaves using the fishbone stitch (page 13). Create the light orange and light pink buds using the floral bud stitch (page 13).

03. Each pansy begins with an indigo center. Stitch the indigo shapes using the long and short stitch (page 14). Leave gaps between the stitches, alternating between long and short lines. Do this step for all the pansy flowers. Add 2 to 3 stitches of light yellow to the center of each flower.

04.

05.

04. Continue stitching the flowers, beginning with the blue pansy. Use the medium blue thread and the long and short stitch. Fill in the petals, angling the stitches vertically towards the top of each the petal. Add a highlight effect to the edges of the two center petals using the light blue thread and the long and short stitch.

05. Switch to the yellow pansy next. Follow the same method as above using the medium yellow as the primary petal color and the light yellow as the accent color. For the red pansy, use the medium red as the primary petal color and the light red as the accent color. Finally, complete the medium purple pansy by using medium purple as the primary color and light purple as the accent color.

06. Remove the water-soluble marker lines and attach the patch, using the iron-on method, to your desired surface, as described on page 119.

Denim Jacket
MAGIC

I definitely saved the best for last. Before I fell madly in love with hats, denim was my favorite embroidery canvas. The first thing I ever embroidered was a denim vest, immediately followed by two denim jackets. This denim dude will add life to your wardrobe and push you to create your largest embroidered piece yet!

Take your favorite fall staple and make it completely unique by adding your artistic touch to it. Don't blend in, stand out by adorning your jacket in a rainbow of vivid threads. Don't be surprised if people ask you where you got such a fashionable piece. Take pride in letting them know you stitched it yourself!

I love how the vibrant colors pop on the dark tone of denim. This design reminds me of being cozy in my fall jacket next to a fire surrounded by my closest friends. For your final project, enjoy stitching your biggest peony yet (page 137).

TIPS FOR CHOOSING A JACKET

I recommend choosing a denim jacket that does not have a thick interior lining. Jackets with a sherpa lining will be difficult to embroider through and will make it very difficult to fit the hoop over the layers of fabric.

ATTACHING AN EMBROIDERY HOOP TO A JACKET

You will use an embroidery hoop for the project in this chapter.

Begin by separating the hoop into two pieces, the inner ring and the outer ring. The outer ring has a metal screw on top that can tighten or loosen the hoop.

Lay the jacket on a flat surface. Place the inner hoop on the inside of the jacket and align it where you would like to embroider. Place the outer hoop on the outside of the jacket and match it up with the inner hoop. Push until the two lock into place. Pull the denim fabric tight on the inside of the hoop and tighten the metal screw. You may need to pull hard to get a flat stitching surface. You may need to move the hoop around the design if the design is larger than the hoop.

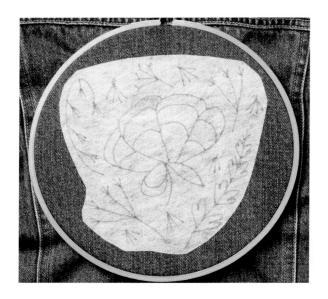

DENIM JACKET PATTERN TRANSFER TUTORIAL

A water-soluble stabilizer is a piece of material that allows you to temporarily affix a pattern to a piece of fabric for the purposes of sewing and embroidery. You can easily draw a design onto the stabilizer, peel off the back like a sticker and stick the stabilizer onto the fabric of your choice. This is super helpful for dark fabrics that do not work with the light box pattern transfer method. It is easy to stitch through the material of the stabilizer. When you're done embroidering, it washes away with water. In this book I use a Sulky Sticky Fabri-Solvy™ brand self-adhesive, fabric-like, water-soluble stabilizer. You can find this and other stabilizers on Amazon or at a craft store.

01. Using scissors, cut out the pattern on page 171.

02. Lay the stabilizer sheet on top of the pattern cutout. You should be able to see the lines easily through the material. If it's hard to see, hold the pattern and stabilizer in front of a bright window or shine a flashlight underneath to illuminate the lines. Transfer the pattern using a water-soluble marker. Use tape to keep the stabilizer still, if needed.

03. Cut the stabilizer out with scissors. Lay your denim jacket on a flat surface and make sure it is wrinkle-free. Peel the stabilizer off of the paper backing and apply it carefully to the fabric. You're ready to stitch!

04. To remove the stabilizer after your embroidery is complete, run warm water over the design. Use your thumb to gently brush away the visible stabilizer material. Blow-dry or air-dry the jacket.

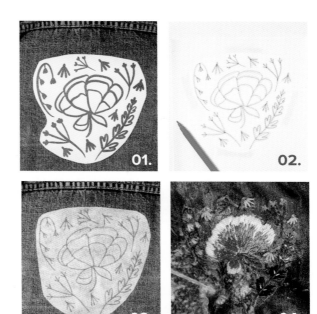

DENIM JACKET EMBROIDERY TIPS

Keep the fabric tight. As you stitch, check the tightness of the fabric. Pull on the fabric on the outside edge of the hoop every so often to create a flat surface inside the hoop.

Keep the thread tight. After every stitch, pull the thread taut so that the stitches aren't loose. The thread may twist; just keep an eye on it. Rotate the needle to untwist it if it is affecting your stitches.

If the chenille needle is hard to get through the fabric, use a thimble or rubber finger grip.

The more you stitch, the more secure your stabilizer will become. In this pattern, I put the greenery first in the tutorial, so the perimeter of the stabilizer is stitched to the fabric. If the stabilizer unsticks, just press it down lightly.

 Lush
PEONY

I wanted the final design in this collection to be extra colorful. So I had to do another pink peony, the big lush flower that dreams are made of! In this project, you create the largest flower in the book. That means lots and lots of the long and short stitch. Take your time, layer the colors to blend them and refer to the photos. Also included in this design is a blue lupine, yellow daisies and some imaginary floral buds—all of my favorites! Keep going once the design is complete: add more colorful flowers and fill up the whole back of the jacket if you'd like!

LEVEL: INTERMEDIATE

MATERIALS

Denim vest or jacket

Template (page 171)

Self-adhesive, fabric-like, water-soluble stabilizer
(My favorite is the Sulky Sticky Fabri-Solvy brand.)

Water-soluble marker

Tape

8-inch (20-cm) wooden embroidery hoop

Size 18 chenille needle

Embroidery scissors

EMBROIDERY THREAD COLORS

Medium green (DMC 905)

Dark hunter green (DMC 3345)

Light orange (DMC 3853)

Light purple (DMC 554)

Medium blue (DMC 3760)

Medium yellow (DMC 725)

Dark blue (DMC 820)

White (DMC 3865)

Dark dusty pink (DMC 3350)

Medium pink (DMC 602)

Light pink (DMC 605)

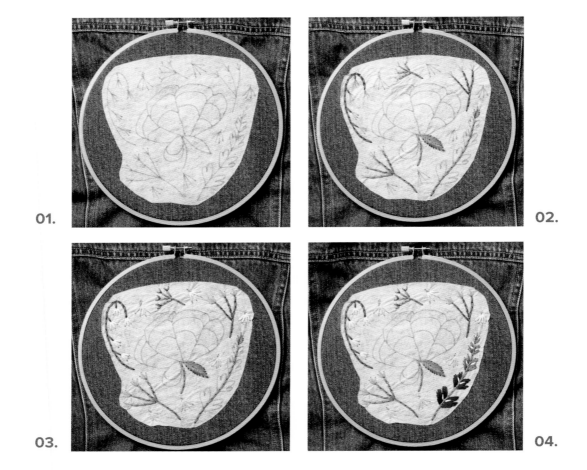

01.
02.
03.
04.

EMBROIDER!

01. Transfer the pattern onto the denim jacket, using the method from the beginning of the chapter (page 134). This entire project will be created using the Double Thread Method (page 9).

02. Stitch the stems with your medium green and dark hunter green threads. The light purple flower and the orange flower on the right side of the design have dark hunter green stems. Use medium green for the remaining stems. Start at the base of the stems and use the backstitch (page 11). Use the fishbone stitch (page 13) in medium green to create the peony leaf and the tip of the lupine.

03. Add flowers onto the floral sprigs using 2 to 3 stitches in the light orange, light purple and medium blue threads. Create the daisies using the daisy shape method (page 12) in medium yellow and light purple with a single light orange stitch for the pollen.

04. The lupine is made up of the dark blue and medium blue threads. Use the satin stitch (page 14) to fill in each flower shape with the stitches angled down and in toward the stem. Add a white stitch to the center of each flower. Continuing with the white thread, add multiple single stitches to the tip of the stem, overlapping the green thread.

05.

06.

07.

05. The peony is made up of 5 petals using dark dusty pink, medium pink and light pink with the long and short stitch (page 14). Start with the dark thread, filling in the bottom shapes and curving around the outside of the flower to create a rounded edge.

06. Continue the peony with the medium pink thread, overlapping the dark pink thread liberally to blend the colors. Use the backstitch in medium pink to outline the inside edges of the petals, to distinguish them from one another.

07. Switch to the light pink thread and continue with the same method. Continue overlapping the thread colors to create a blended, painterly look. Make the edge of each petal clean and uniform. Use the backstitch to create lines in light pink, meeting up with the medium pink lines between the petals.

08. Remove the pattern transfer paper, as described on page 135. Your denim jacket is ready to be worn!

TEMPLATES

STRAWBERRY SWEETHEARTS HAT (PAGE 21)

WILDFLOWER MAGIC HAT (PAGE 25)

1   2   3

BLOOMIN' CACTUS HAT (PAGE 29)

1   2

BLOSSOMING ALASKA WILDFLOWERS HAT (PAGE 33)

1

2

CALIFORNIA DREAMIN' POPPIES HAT (PAGE 37)

1

2

ECHINACEA IN BLOOM HAT (PAGE 41)

1

2

MUSHROOM PARTY HAT (PAGE 45)

1   2

SWEET FLORIDA ORANGES HAT (PAGE 49)

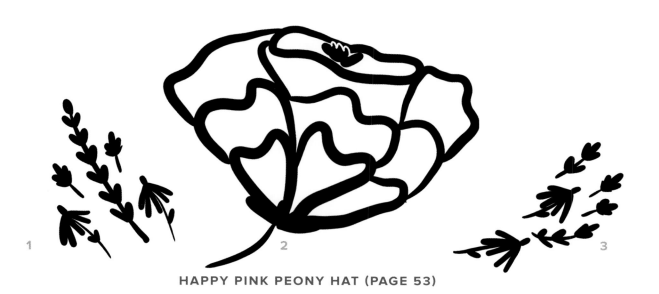

1   2   3

HAPPY PINK PEONY HAT (PAGE 53)

1   2   3

UNFURLED FERN HAT (PAGE 57)

1   2   3

DAISY DUDES BANDANA (PAGE 65)

1

2

3

LOVELY LAVENDER BANDANA
(PAGE 67)

MINI MUSHROOMS BANDANA (PAGE 71)

1

3

2

RED POPPY PALS BANDANA (PAGE 75)

1

2

3

LIL' LEMON SLICES BANDANA
(PAGE 79)

LUSH LUPINE
FANNY PACK
(PAGE 91)

1

2

3

BABY BIRDS-OF-PARADISE BANDANA (PAGE 83)

TROPICAL MONSTERA FANNY PACK (PAGE 93)

RADIANT SUNFLOWER FANNY PACK (PAGE 97)

SPROUTING COFFEE PLANT TOTE (PAGE 105)

FRESH FRUIT TOTE (PAGE 109)

COLORFUL SUCCULENTS TOTE (PAGE 113)

SNAPDRAGON RAINBOW PATCH
(PAGE 123)

OVERFLOWING POTHOS PLANTER PATCH
(PAGE 125)

PANSY PALS PATCH (PAGE 129)

LUSH PEONY DENIM JACKET (PAGE 137)

ACKNOWLEDGMENTS

Sometimes I feel like my life is a dream come true. I am so grateful for every creative opportunity I have had, and writing this book is by far my biggest creative accomplishment yet.

I want to thank my husband Jesse for supporting me, not only through this writing process, but through all of my creative whims and passions. Thank you for every dinner, every pep talk and every dance party. You steady me and help me keep things in perspective in the most important ways. This book, this life, this person I am, wouldn't be the same without you. I love you.

Thank you to my loving and supportive family, for always cheering for me throughout my creative career. A special thank-you to my dad who always beams at me the way that any daughter would be lucky to be looked at. Thank you for the endless love and for passing on your creative genes.

Thank you to my incredible community of friends far and wide for supporting my embroidery journey from the very start: from buying hats and kits to sharing and wearing my work. And for always checking in and letting me disappear into my work for a few months.

Thank you to Emily for always listening through joyful and chaotic times. For always lifting me up, for holding space for me and for being my sounding board for every creative thought, big or small. I discover so much about myself and what is important to me through conversations with you. Thank you to Dana for being endlessly full of love and support. It is a joy to see myself and the world through your positive lens. Thank you to all of the Murray Hill fam, for being my chosen family. Thank you to my long-distance best friends Lindsey and Caitlin for being there for me from high school until now, always supporting my creative spirit.

Extra special thank-you to the incredible team at Page Street Publishing, especially my editor Jenna Fagan. Your patience knows no bounds and I seriously appreciate all of your expertise and input during this process. This wouldn't exist without you, and I am so proud of what we have created together.

ABOUT THE AUTHOR

Lexi Mire Brantman is an embroidery artist living in Jacksonville, Florida. She started her embroidery business in 2017 after her embroidered hats went viral within the embroidery community on Instagram and Pinterest. Now, 20,000 followers and more than 1,000 orders later, Lexi has created a striking, signature style of modern embroidery that is easy and fun to learn.

Along with stitching for customers, Lexi also provides embroidery education, including PDFs and DIY embroidery kits so that curious creatives can make something beautiful and unique. Lexi has been featured on the Brown Paper Bag blog and Babes Who Hustle blog. She has taught workshops in her community and spoken on panels about being a woman in the freelance world. When she's not stitching, she is the social media manager for a local nonprofit and a loving cat mom.

INDEX

A

A Garden of Floral Patches, 116–131

B

Baby Birds-of-Paradise, 83–85, 159

backstitch, 11

bandana pattern transfer tutorial, 62–63

bandanas, 60–85

bandana tips, 62–63

Bloomin' Cactus, 28–31, 143

Blossoming Alaska Wildflowers, 32–35, 143

C

California Dreamin' Poppies, 36–39, 145

Colorful and Creative Bandanas, 60–85

Colorful Succulents, 112–115, 167

D

Daisy Dudes, 64–66, 149

daisy shape method, 12

denim jacket, 132–139

Denim Jacket Magic, 132–139

denim jacket pattern transfer tutorial, 134–135

denim jacket tips, 134–135

double thread method, 9

E

Echinacea in Bloom, 40–43, 145

Embroidery Basics, 8–9

embroidery hoop (how to use), 8, 18

F

fanny pack pattern transfer tutorial, 88–89

fanny packs, 86–99

fanny pack tips, 88–89

finishing stitches, 9

fishbone stitch, 13

floral bud stitch, 13

Flowery Fanny Packs, 86–99

Fresh Fruit, 108–111, 165

H

Happy Pink Peony, 52–55, 147

hat pattern transfer tutorial, 18–19

hats, 16–59

hat tips, 18–19

L

Lil' Lemon Slices, 79–82, 157

long and short stitch, 14

Lovely Lavender, 67–70, 151

Lush Lupine, 90–92, 159

Lush Peony, 136–139, 171

M

Mini Mushrooms, 71–74, 153

Mushroom Party, 44–47, 145

N

neck scarf, 63

needle threading methods, 8–9

O

Overflowing Pothos Planter, 125–127, 169

P

Pansy Pals, 128–131, 169

patches, 116–131

patch pattern tutorial, 118–119

patch tips, 118–120

R

Radiant Sunflower, 96–99, 161

Red Poppy Pals, 75–78, 155

S

satin stitch, 14

single thread method, 8–9

Snapdragon Rainbow, 122–124, 169

Sprouting Coffee Plant, 104–107, 163

Stitch Guide, 11–15

Strawberry Sweethearts, 20–23, 141

Sweet Florida Oranges, 48–51, 147

Sweetly Stitched Floral Hats, 16–59

T

Templates, 141–171

Too Cute Tote Bags, 100–115

tote bag pattern transfer tutorial, 103

tote bags, 100–115

tote bag tips, 102–103

Tropical Monstera, 93–95, 161

U

Unfurled Fern, 56–59, 149

W

whipstitch, 15

Wildflower Magic, 24–27, 141

Z

zipper pouch, 88

Make Everyday Accessories Pop
WITH A TOUCH OF STITCHED STYLE

"The humble hat and basic bandana can become dazzling works of art, as Lexi demonstrates time and again. Her projects are ideal for the crafter that wants to mix things up and make their creativity a statement-making part of their wardrobe."

—SARA BARNES, creator of Brown Paper Bag and author of *Embroidered Life*

"Lexi has created a charming bundle of vibrant embroidery projects that are perfect for beginners and bursting with joy!"

—EMILLIE FERRIS, creator of Emillie Ferris Embroidery

"Not only will you be able to personalize your outfit with Lexi's stylish designs; you will also enjoy creating something precious by learning some cool embroidery skills."

—IREM YAZICI, creator of Baobap and author of *Tiny Stitches*

With Lexi Mire Brantman's creative embroidery tutorials, you can turn your clothing and accessories into wearable art. Choose from over 25 of Lexi's whimsical, bestselling designs for baseball hats, totes, bandanas, fanny packs, patches and jean jackets to add a trendy bohemian touch to your wardrobe. You can also get creative and adapt these patterns onto all kinds of clothing, including flannels and jeans, and even home accessories like tablecloths, tea towels, pillowcases and napkins.

You'll love adding floral charm to your favorite baseball cap with patterns like Bloomin' Cactus and California Dreamin' Poppies. Shop the local farmers' market in style with a too-cute tote bag decorated with Fresh Fruit. To top it all off, turn your jean jacket into a statement piece by embroidering it with a bright, vibrant Lush Peony.

Lexi's clear project instructions and step-by-step photos make stitching these patterns a breeze, even if you've never embroidered before. Her easy, modern style is achievable for beginners and exciting for experienced embroiderers alike, so everyone can enjoy adding a fun personalized touch to their wardrobe.

LEXI MIRE BRANTMAN is the founder of Mire Made Embroidery, where she sells her embroidery art and teaches others how to stitch using her signature modern style. She has been featured on the Brown Paper Bag and Babes Who Hustle websites, amongst other publications. She lives in Jacksonville, Florida.

Page Street
PUBLISHING CO.

CRAFTS & HOBBIES / Needlework / Embroidery $21.99

ISBN 978-1-64567-122-0

52199>

9 781645 671220